The Crucified Guru

The Crucified Guru

*An Experiment in
Cross-Cultural Christology*

M. Thomas Thangaraj

Abingdon Press
Nashville

THE CRUCIFIED GURU
AN EXPERIMENT IN CROSS-CULTURAL CHRISTOLOGY

This book is printed on acid-free recycled paper.

Library of Congress Cataloging-in-Publication Data

Thangaraj, M. Thomas (Melchizedec Thomas)
    The crucified guru: an experiment in cross-cultural Christology/
M. Thomas Thangaraj.
    p. cm.
    ISBN 0-687-10008-9 (alk. paper)
    1. Jesus Christ—Person and offices.   2. Gurus.   3. Christianity
and other religions—Hinduism.   4. Hinduism—Relations—
Christianity.   5. Saiva Siddhanta—Doctrines.   I. Title.
BT205.T47   1994
232—dc20   94-25502
                                                                              CIP

94 95 96 97 98 99 00 01 02 03—10 9 8 7 6 5 4 3 2 1

MANUFACTURED IN THE UNITED STATES OF AMERICA

To
Cecilia

ACKNOWLEDGMENTS

Several years of my own thinking, and the insights of several of my teachers, colleagues, and students have gone into the making of this book. Since the time I began to formulate this project as a doctoral dissertation many have helped me on this christological journey, and I want to gratefully acknowledge their contribution to this work. My special thanks are due:

To Professors Gordon D. Kaufman and John B. Carman of Harvard University, who taught and helped me to think clearly and constructively;

To my friends Jerome Soneson, Melanie May, and Luis Rivera, who provided me a community of conversation and support during the initial stages of research;

To Professor S. Gangadharan, Head of the Department of Saiva Siddhanta, Madurai-Kamaraj University, Madurai, India, and other Saivite friends, who willingly shared their faith with me and welcomed me into their world of Saivite piety and philosophy;

To Bob Ratcliff, my editor at Abingdon Press, who read through the manuscript with care and suggested valuable changes toward precision, clarity, and beauty in the text; to Steven Cox, my copyeditor at Abingdon, who edited the manuscript with meticulous care to maintain accuracy and consistency in language and other details; and finally

To my wife, Cecilia, and our children, Raja and Naveena, who kept teaching me during the research and writing that thinking and writing should always be accompanied by loving and caring.

NOTES ON THE
TRANSLITERATION OF TAMIL WORDS

The transliteration of Tamil words used in this volume has been done in partial accordance with the standard form as it appears in *Library of Congress, Cataloging Service Bulletin* (no. 120, Winter 1977, p. 43). The following exceptions are made:

1) All diacritical marks are omitted, for two reasons. First, these marks are understandable only to those whose familiarity with the Tamil language renders them capable of recognizing the Tamil equivalents even without the diacritical marks. Second, these marks make reading the text difficult for a reader who is not familiar with the Tamil language.

2) Words that are familiar in the context of several other Indian languages are written in the more popular Sanskrit, not in the Tamil. They are: avatar, bhakti, carya, diksa, guru, jnana, kriya, marga, maya, mudra, sastra, siddhar, sisya, sutra, and yoga.

3) The following terms are not italicized, because of their familiarity and frequency: agama, bhakti, guru, guru-sisya, saiva, sastra, siddhanta, sisya, Siva, Sivam, sutra, and veda.

4) To enable the reader easily to recognize the Sanskrit equivalents, certain Tamil words are written with the letter "s" instead of "c." They are: asat, pasam, pasu, sahaja, sakala, sakalar, sakamarga, salokya, samipya, sangam, sanmarga, sarguru, sarupya, sat, satti or sakti, sayujya, and siva.

CONTENTS

FOREWORD

In a familiar passage in Acts, Paul is portrayed as speaking with philosophers and others in Athens. He begins his remarks by referring to an altar he had noted as he walked around the city looking at various "objects of . . . worship." Among them, he says, "I found . . . an altar with the inscription, 'To an unknown god.' What therefore you worship as unknown, this I proclaim to you" (17:23). He goes on then to speak of this unknown God as the "God who made the world and everything in it" (24), and he eventually suggests that some of the Greeks' own poets had also spoken of this God "in [whom] we live and move and have our being" (28).

This speech of Paul at the Areopagus has long been regarded as a kind of model of the way in which the Christian message can be presented in cultures in which it was previously unknown. Paul is portrayed as one who takes great pains to make his message as intelligible and clear to his listeners as possible: In his speech he takes up their non-Christian artifacts and concepts, meanings and values, and then builds on these as he makes his Christian appeal. This approach, of course, has some inherent dangers. If the similarity of the Christian message to what is familiar is too much emphasized, its radical distinctiveness—and thus its unique importance—will be obscured; and the whole point of the preaching will be lost. The degree to which and the way in which the Christian gospel should or can be presented in concepts and symbols already heavily freighted with non-Christian meanings and emphases are very delicate matters.

It is hardly surprising that these important theological issues were much discussed during the nineteenth and twentieth centuries of worldwide missionary expansion of Christianity, and that they remain of great concern today as Christians in non-Western cultures attempt to free themselves of the Westernized versions of Christian faith with which the missionaries almost always left them. Can "authentic" Christian faith be expressed in and through "pagan" religious symbols and concepts? Is it not necessary—if we are to avoid compromising the "essentials" of the Christian message—that we retain as our norm the language of orthodoxy, worked out in the early history of the churches? Or is this so-called orthodoxy itself so colored—indeed, distorted—by the particularities of the (Greek and Roman) pagan philosophical and religious languages and attitudes in which it was initially formulated, that it can quite properly be largely disregarded in settings where other significantly different moral and religious values and meanings have been formative? This latter position certainly seems to have some immediate plausibility, but if one accepts it, does it not become virtually impossible to continue making clear distinctions between true and false (or misleading) forms of Christianity? Will we not, then, find ourselves on a "slippery slope" with no way to avoid falling off the edge?

Many Western Christians, from the beginnings of the missionary movement to the present-day worldwide ecumenical movement, have been especially concerned about these last questions. Only in recent years—as it has become increasingly recognized that Western political, cultural, and religious imperialism profoundly compromised the missionary movement, and as it has become clear that the formulas of Christian orthodoxy were themselves heavily shaped by particular philosophical and religious ideas and languages of an ancient historical period as parochial in most respects as any other—has it become possible to think about the (potential) universality of the Christian movement in a new way: a way that builds on a new understanding of the theological significance of the religious pluralism of humankind. Instead of continuing to fight desperately against the massive pluralism of human cultures and religions in the name of what is believed to be universal Christian truth, we are now beginning to see that each cultural and religious tradition—in its own distinctive way—may have something uniquely significant to contribute to the understanding of Christian faith; and that precisely through its translation into concepts and symbols formerly seen as "alien" and "dangerous" new dimensions of its meaning may thus come into view. From this perspective, one can see, it is a mistake to suppose that the universality of Christianity resides in the orthodoxy of some bygone age; on the contrary, it is something still coming into being—something still being created!—through the processes of cultural and linguistic diffusion, as new aspects and dimensions of human life and experience become incorporated into the continuing growth of the Christian vision of the world and the human.

The present book, in which Professor M. Thomas Thangaraj examines carefully how the Indian concept of "guru" (as used by Tamil Saivites) can contribute significantly to christological thinking today—not only in India but in the West as well—makes this point clear in a straightforward but quite profound way. After exploring (in chapters 2 and 3) the meanings and uses of the concept "guru" in various Indian settings (including its somewhat infrequent use by Christians as a title for Jesus), he sketches with subtlety and care a christology informed principally by this distinctly Indian symbol. When the traditional Jesus-story (in which Jesus is often presented as a "teacher" or "rabbi") is interpreted in terms of the notion of *guru* (the Indian word for a religious teacher), the understandings of both Jesus and "guru" are significantly affected: on the one hand, Jesus comes to be seen as the revelation or "presence" of God in a much more open, less restrictive way, than is suggested by the traditional notion of incarnation (or the Indian notion of *avatar*); and, on the other hand, the concept of guru itself becomes transformed significantly as it is filled concretely by Jesus' distinctive teachings and practices, and especially by the story of his crucifixion-resurrection. One can see from Professor Thangaraj's discussion how much more intelligible—and more impressive—this sort of presentation of the Jesus-story must be in the Indian setting, than are versions putting heavy emphasis on the traditional incarnational formulas, which have very little resonance there.

Moreover (and this may come as a surprise to many European and American Christians), the open christology which the symbol "guru," as Professor Thangaraj works it out, makes possible, is also able—without diminishing the unique significance of Christ—to bypass many of the problems which modern Western Christians confront as they attempt to comprehend traditional christological talk about special metaphysical natures, essences, substances, and so on. Thus, it turns out that the intelligibility and meaning of Christian faith for many of us Westerners, living in our modern-postmodern world, is also enhanced by the christological reflection facilitated when the concept of guru is brought into the discussion. *The Crucified Guru* presents us with a remarkable example of the deepening and widening toward a truer universality that can occur as Christian reflection moves into and incorporates into itself fresh ways of thinking about the human condition under God, ways of thinking enabled and encouraged by new (previously non-Christian) linguistic and cultural contexts. *The Crucified Guru,* thus, is as important for the American and European theological scene as it is for India. It is the kind of book that can help us see more clearly the limitations and relativity of not only the traditional christological language that we have inherited, but of our current christological thinking as well; and it can thus open us Westerners to a wider vision of what Christian faith can mean in the modern-postmodern religiously and culturally plural world of which we today are increasingly becoming aware. I am delighted that it is being published in an American edition, and I hope that it has a wide reading in both East and West.

Gordon D. Kaufman
Mallinckrodt Professor of Divinity
Harvard Divinity School

What is required . . . today is courage rather than cautiousness, a spirit of adventure rather than one of conformity, a complete loyalty to Christ rather than desire for prestige in the Church. Hesitation would mean theological paralysis.

Stanley J. Samartha

CHAPTER 1

INTRODUCTION

I am a bilingual person. I began my education in my mother tongue of Tamil, one of the four main South Indian languages. Soon I began to learn the English language as well. Both my undergraduate and graduate education took place in English. Though my theological education was only in English, as a presbyter of the Church of South India I preached Sunday after Sunday in the Tamil language. When I joined the faculty of Tamilnadu Theological Seminary, Madurai, India, I began to *teach* theology in Tamil. Because there were not enough Christian theological books in the Tamil language, I had to depend on works written in English. It was not always easy to explicate the ideas of Western theologians in the Tamil language. For example, explaining Tillich's idea of "ultimate concern" to my students was both a challenging and a frustrating experience. I soon discovered that discussing the Tamil concept of *parruruti* (literally, strong commitment) and then moving to Tillich's idea of ultimate concern was much easier and more helpful than the other way round. It was an exciting experience thus to travel back and forth between English and Tamil. This was not simply true of my educational activities; it was true of my home as well, where my wife and I, and our two children spoke to one another in a language that was a creative and imaginative mixture of English and Tamil.

I am a bilingual person on other counts too, if one gives a wider meaning to the word "lingual." Though I began to speak in these two languages quite early on, it was only in 1964 that I came to an awareness that I was beginning to *think* and *dream* in English. At that point I became more than a bilingual person; I became a self-consciously bi*cultural* person. I could grasp and enjoy humor in both cultural contexts—Tamil culture and cultures informed by English. I could listen to and enjoy both Beethoven and Thiagaraja (a South Indian classical composer). I began to live in two worlds— the worlds of Tamil culture and Western culture.

I have also inherited two religious languages—Hindu and Christian. My ancestors were Hindus who nearly two hundred years ago decided to embrace the Christian faith. Though they made every effort to devise a uniquely Christian religious language, one markedly different from that of their Hindu counterparts, they did not fully succeed, thanks to Tamil Christian poets and hymn-writers. The Tamil Christian hymns were bilingual, in the sense that they used Hindu religious terms, ideas, and symbols side-by-side with Judeo-Christian terms and concepts. For example, Vedanayagam Sastriar, one of the leading Tamil Christian hymn-writers, addresses God as *parabrahmaekova* in one of his hymns.[1] This phrase is a combination of *brahman* (the Hindu term for Ultimate Reality) and *ekova* (the transliterated form of YHWH). There were also other liturgical and social practices among Christians that nurtured the bilingual religiosity of Tamil Christians. Though I had not consciously engaged in this bilingual religious discourse in my early life, as a theology student and theology teacher I came to discover how bilingual I was, and how my theology was informed by both religious traditions. My involvement in programs of interreligious dialogue between Hindus and Christians heightened my awareness of this bilingual character. Today I find myself thinking, speaking, and writing in both Hindu and Christian theological languages.

Another area of bilinguality I have inherited is that of poet and theologian. For the last thirty years I have been engaged in the exciting task of writing hymns in Tamil.[2] At the same time, I have been trained in the academy to speak a language not always as imaginative as that of poetry and hymnody. It is indeed a strange experience to be imagining God in Tamil and discussing theology in English. While my theology professors did teach me that theology was poetry, they also taught me that clarity in argumentation, preciseness in expression, and rigor in logic were equally as important as the poetic imagination. Therefore, I find myself speaking yet another set of dual languages—the language of the poet and that of the academician. In other words, I try to combine the two tasks of *preaching* theology to a worshiping congregation and *teaching* theology to a community of students.

Finally, my bilingual status also means that I employ both the language of contextualization and the language of globalization in my theological task. When I joined the faculty of Tamilnadu Theological Seminary in 1971, the call to contextualize theology and theological education was being heard loud and clear in India, through the efforts of both the theological leadership in India and the Theological Education Fund of the World Council of Churches. Theologians in India were beginning to articulate a truly "Indian Christian theology." In 1969 Robin Boyd, a missionary theologian in India, published a book entitled *An Introduction to Indian Christian Theology,* which was a historical survey of the contextual theological attempts in India from the sixteenth century onward.[3] This book helped bring "to light the continuity of the hidden stream of living theology which has been flowing in India."[4] Thus contextualization meant for me and other theologians in India the task of constructing a theology that was relevant and meaningful to the Indian experience; such a theology would seek neither to be guided nor to be judged by the theological enterprise in the West. In this vein the Indian Christian theologian P. Chenchiah wrote:

> Let it be clearly understood that we accept nothing as obligatory save Christ. Church doctrine and dogma, whether from the West or from the past, whether from Apostles or from modern critics, are to be tested before they are accepted.[5]

These attempts at contextualization in Indian Christianity represented the ways in which Indian Christian theologians were beginning to question the false sense of universalism that lay behind Western theological writings. The false universalism to which I refer views European theology as the benchmark, and very often as normative, for all theological reflection and construction in India and elsewhere. Therefore contextualization was a reaction against a domineering and subjugating type of "universalizing"; it was a way of joining the global discussion without allowing oneself to be dominated by theologies in the West.

When I joined the faculty of Candler School of Theology, Emory University, Atlanta, Georgia, in 1988, I came to be closely associated with a different task, namely, the globalization of theology and theological education. I was invited to teach in the area of world Christianity, which involved interpreting the life and work of churches in other parts of the world to the American students. As early as 1980 the Association of Theological Schools in the United States and Canada had formed a committee to examine the "internationalization" (as it was called at that time) of theological education.

> A new consciousness of the worldwide church and the interdependence of humanity had begun to raise questions about some of the assumptions on which theological education in the Western world was built. Cross-cultural awareness made those in the West conscious that their culture and religious view of the world were no longer normative. Theological schools in North America were faced with the challenge of educating students who would have a global awareness of the church and of the world.[6]

From that point on, theological schools in the United States have attempted to engage in globalization in several differing ways.

My own role in the effort to globalize theological education has been to promote a bilingual conversation between theologies in the United States and those outside the United States. Walter Brueggemann describes the task of globalization this way:

> The process of globalization as it concerns critical theological thought is much like the process whereby we emerge from our tribal realities, peek over the top of the hill, and discover in the next valley people who are also "doing it" ("it" being theology). . . . As we watch the people in the next valley do their theological work, we may over time modify our ways of doing it in light of what we see over there.[7]

It is becoming clear that the idea of globalization has really caught on in Western theological circles. For example, we have seen a significant interest in christologies from Latin America, Asia, Africa, and other non-Western parts of the world. The list of books published in this area is impressive. They include: José Miguez Bonino, *Faces* of Jesus: *Latin American Christologies;* Anton Wessels, *Images of Jesus: How Jesus Is Perceived and Portrayed in Non-European Cultures;* Robert J. Schreiter (ed.), *Faces of Jesus in Africa;* Priscilla Pope Levison and John R. Levison, *Jesus in Global Contexts;* and R. S. Sugirtharajah (ed.), *Asian Faces of Jesus.*[8] The titles themselves are very revealing of the kind of globalization that Brueggemann describes.

The interesting feature here is that I find myself on both sides of the hill, because I do theology in both "valleys"—Tamilnadu in India and Georgia in the United States.[9] While I ask my students in India to be intensely and purposely involved in the local context, I plead with my students in the United States to look beyond their horizon and get a glimpse of what is happening in other parts of the world. In this yet further sense of the term, I am a bilingual person.

The kind of bilingual or cross-cultural character of thinking and acting I refer to here is not peculiar to me as a person. It is increasingly becoming the feature of communities, churches, and societies around the world. The world we live in today is an interconnected and interdependent one where the line between what is local (or contextual) and what is global is disappearing. The global has invaded the local and the local has entered the global.[10] To give a mundane example, the growth in the number of ethnic restaurants in cities of the United States signals such an entry of the local into the global. The principal cities of the world, whether Bombay, London, New York, or Tokyo, all exhibit this interweaving of the local and the global. The languages spoken in these cities are manifold. The places of worship holding to differing religious traditions are many and varied. Yet this is not simply true of the leading cities alone. Even the remote villager in India is aware of the wider world in which we live today, thanks to the explosion of communication technology. Youth in Madurai, South India, discuss the marvelous choreography of American basketball stars while listening to the music of Michael Jackson or Mariah Carey. Both men and women in Madras use Tamil or another Indian language at home but speak English to their friends at the mall and to their colleagues in the workplace. Young people in Atlanta are attending Buddhist meditation sessions and taking yoga classes. Robert Schreiter describes this emerging global culture as characterized by American cola drinks, athletic and casual clothing, and American movie and television entertainment. It is a culture sent virtually everywhere, but received in considerably different fashions. For example, "Dynasty" is watched differently in Lagos than in Los Angeles. . . . The universality is both real and unreal at the same time. It is real inasmuch as it is found everywhere; it is unreal in that what it signifies means different things in the reception of the local culture.[11]

Moreover, the international political and economic situation demands a bilingual existence today. Every political issue and every economic question is a tapestry of local and global concerns. The word "globalization" has found its place in art, business, politics, economics, and trade. Business corporations everywhere are training their managers and workers in the art of negotiating in the global marketplace. This means that being cross-cultural or bilingual is no longer a luxury; it has become a necessity.

This interpenetration of the local and the global can be enhanced and put to creative use only within a posture of dialogue—dialogue between contextualization and globalization, between Hindu and Christian ways of thinking and articulating, between Tamil and English, between Indian and American cultures. This book will present such a dialogue within the boundaries of christology. What I attempt here is a christology that initiates a dialogue between the different "languages" I have just described. I am attempting to construct a christology that is local-global, Tamil-English, aesthetic-academic, and Hindu-Christian. This is possible because christology has always been an exercise in dialogue. Did it not begin with the dialogue between Jesus and his disciples on the way to Caesarea Philippi, when he asked his disciples, "Who do people say that I am?" (Mark 8:27)? Even today dialogue is that which sustains and enriches any christological experiment, as the title of a recent work on christology by Robert F. Berkey and Sarah A. Edwards—*Christology in Dialogue*—demonstrates.[12] In the opening chapter, the editor rightly notes that

"dialogue" is the key word, and it carries our conviction that Christology loses its vitality when it is not so engaged. Whether in their first-century or in their Chalcedonian or Enlightenment clothing,

Christological formulations have always fallen short of finality. . . .
Christology is never final but always in dialogue.[13]

The kind of dialogue that I am suggesting here is important
because in its absence christology will end up either as a narrow
parochial vision of Christ or as a deceptively universal portrayal of
Christ. In other words, a christology that is self-consciously local
needs to take the global dimension seriously so that it does not end
up as tribal and parochial. Similarly, a christology that does not
realize the contextual character of its articulation promotes a false
sense of universalism and thus assumes that it is applicable to all
situations, times, and places—a problem that runs deep throughout
the christologies in the West. Western theologians had assumed that
their christological articulations were context-free and thus applicable to global situations. One senses that Western theologians have
viewed Christ as "out there" so to speak—embodied in the texts of
the New Testament or the formulations of the ecclesial creeds—and
that therefore one's task is simply to translate this reality into one's
own mother tongue.

This false sense of universalism, coupled with a christological
positivism, has come under severe attack from all sides. The dissat-
isfaction with the traditional ways of doing christology has come in
at least three different forms. Let us discuss each of them so that our
own christological project might address the issues brought to the
surface by these protests.

INADEQUACY OF INCARNATIONAL LANGUAGE

When *The Myth of God Incarnate* was published in 1977, it stirred
up a great controversy among theologians in Britain and throughout
the world.[14] The contributors to the volume detect several difficulties
in articulating the significance of Jesus the Christ through the idea
of incarnation. By incarnational faith they mean "a description of
Christianity as a faith whose central tenet affirms the incarnation of
God in the particular individual Jesus of Nazareth."[15] They go on to
add that this faith affirms that "Jesus of Nazareth is unique in the
precise sense that, while being fully man, it is true of him, and of him

25

alone, that he is also fully God, the Second Person of the co-equal Trinity."[16] With this definition of incarnational faith, Maurice Wiles, in the opening chapter, asks whether there could be a Christianity without this idea of incarnation. For both Wiles and others it is possible to explicate the meaning of Christ without incarnational language.

The problems these theologians find in the doctrine of incarnation are many. First, they point out that the mythical language of incarnation is not intelligible to modern humans, because it is sustained by a world view that is no longer widely accepted. We who are shaped by a radical historical consciousness tend to be skeptical about myths and mythical language. As Frances Young, one of the theologians, writes,

> In the Western world, both popular culture and the culture of the intelligentsia has come to be dominated by the human and natural sciences to such an extent that supernatural causation or intervention in the affairs of this world has become, for the majority of people, simply incredible.[17]

Second, it is by no means self-evident that the New Testament and other early church sources can support the kind of incarnational doctrine that has come into prominence in Christian theology. Third, the idea of incarnation has a built-in tendency toward a docetic view of Christ. However one may try to emphasize the humanity of Jesus, ultimately the incarnate Logos becomes the more important part of Jesus' personality, and thus his humanity ends up as a mere appearance. Furthermore, a closer examination of the idea of incarnation leads often to "the blind alleys paradox and illogicality."[18] Finally, the doctrine of incarnation is also seen as leading to very exclusive claims about Jesus that hinder Christian believers from relating to people of other religious traditions with generosity and hospitality.[19]

I will not here go into the several kinds of objections raised to the way the authors of *The Myth of God Incarnate* attempted to construct a christology without the idea of incarnation.[20] But one should note that the discussion initiated by that debate continues even today. For example, there are those who question the adequacy of incarnational language. Schubert Ogden, for one, lists the difficulties with the doctrine of incarnation as outmoded conceptuality, inadequacy in explaining the talk of Jesus as God and human, and the tendency toward docetism and kenoticism.[21] On the other hand there are those who continue to criticize this questioning of the idea of incarnation. Brian O. McDermott complains that once Hick's reinterpretation of incarnation is accepted, "one must ask whether the very center has not been taken out of Christianity, and one is dealing with a religion of one's own invention."[22] A much more critical and interesting evaluation of *The Myth of God Incarnate* has come from theologians like Jürgen Moltmann and Gordon Kaufman, who are disturbed, not by the mythical character of the idea of incarnation, but rather by the mistaken linking of incarnation with the single historical person of Jesus of Nazareth.[23]

The problem of the doctrine of incarnation has been discussed by Indian Christian theologians as well. Yet for these theologians, the problem is not the mythical character of the idea of incarnation, but the unique and once-for-all character of Christic incarnation in the face of a multiplicity of incarnations in the Hindu religious tradition. V. Chakkarai addresses precisely this issue in his book, *Jesus the Avatar* (the term *avatar* is the closest Hindu equivalent to the Christian idea of incarnation).[24] Nor is this discussion limited to Christian theologians. Hindu theologians challenged one another over the idea of incarnation in South India from the eleventh to the thirteenth century C.E. It is within this intra-Hindu discussion that one discovers the concept of guru; the point of this book is to demonstrate that this religious concept can be of considerable help to us today in explicating the significance of Jesus the Christ.

INSUFFICIENCY OF DOCTRINAL ORTHODOXY

When the English edition of Gustavo Gutiérrez's *A Theology of Liberation: History, Politics, and Salvation* was published in 1973, a fresh approach to the task of theologizing was introduced.[25] This approach saw Christian theology "as a critical reflection on praxis," rather than simply reflection on, and reiteration of, the doctrines of the Christian church. Faithfulness to doctrinal orthodoxy was found to be a criterion that stifled creativity, legitimated oppression, and was irrelevant to the concerns of the poor and the marginalized in the various nations of the world. Gutiérrez posited orthopraxis, or right action (as opposed to right doctrine), as the criterion for a relevant and meaningful Christian theology.

Two other Latin American theologians—Jon Sobrino and Leonardo Boff—also have exposed the inadequacy of doctrinal orthodoxy in constructing an authentic christology.[26] The christologies of Sobrino and Boff are organized around the idea that a christology, if it is to bear fruit in praxis, should envision Jesus Christ as the one who liberates people from the chains of oppression, exploitation, and marginalization. It is only "through Jesus that we learn what liberation is and how it is to be achieved."[27] Sobrino and Boff have been joined by a host of Latin American theologians in explicating a liberation christology. Though there are subtle differences between the various Latin American theologians, the common thread that unites them all is the centrality of the concept of *liberation* (seen primarily in socioeconomic and political terms) and the emphasis on the historical Jesus. The return to the historical Jesus, for Latin American theologians, is not the same as the "quest" or the "new quest" for the historical Jesus in the nineteenth and twentieth centuries respectively. The earlier quests failed to grasp "the historical concreteness and the specificity" of Jesus by separating the historical Jesus completely from the Christ of faith.[28] The specificity of the historical Jesus lies in the fact that he finds himself in a situation of oppression and a longing for liberation (not unlike the situation in Latin America), and his history expresses "clearly and unmistakably the need for achieving liberation, the meaning of liberation, and the way to attain it."[29] In other words, the "historical" Jesus is in fact the history of Jesus viewed through the categories of oppression and liberation. Both these concerns undermine the importance of orthodoxy and accentuate the criterion of orthopraxis. In the words of another Latin American theologian,

> The locus of encounter with Jesus is the road he himself trod. We find him when we "join him on the way." For the relevance of Jesus' praxis invites us not to repeat his history, but precisely to make our own. The handling of his history is not the womb of nostalgia, but the mega-

phone that educates us to genuine historical freedom. Unless our titles for him make Jesus rich with our praxis, they will never be more than fetishes and idols.[30]

The emphasis on orthopraxis has not gone unchallenged. Some see it as anti-intellectual and simplistic. For example, John Macquarrie writes that

> it is doubtful if one can simply claim that orthopraxis takes precedence over orthodoxy. The relation between belief and action is very complex, and certainly has some elements of reciprocity . . . emphasis on action rather than thinking occasionally leads to something close to anti-intellectualism.[31]

While such criticism has persisted, the idea of orthopraxis has caught the attention of theologians all around the world, and "liberation" christologies have sprung up in different parts of the globe. For example, theologians in the continent of Africa and African American theologians in the United States have both called for a return to history and praxis. James Cone would argue that a proper reading of the New Testament (i.e., a good understanding of the historical Jesus) inevitably shows Jesus as the "Oppressed One whose earthly existence was bound up with the oppressed of the land," and helps us to recognize him as the Black Messiah and Liberator.[32] Laurenti Magesa, an African theologian, makes a similar affirmation:

> When we speak of Jesus as Liberator, then we refer to his assurance of solidarity with us, particularly but not exclusively as church, in the struggle—his struggle—to diminish poverty among the masses of the people. . . . We refer to his commitment to forming the rule of God by refusing to accept as right sinful structures of religious or civil domination, corruption, and tribalism.[33]

Whereas Latin American liberation christologies concentrate on the class struggle in the process of liberation, the African and African American theologians recognize and highlight the issues of classism *and* racism in the struggle for liberation.

29

Another group of theologians that has questioned the adequacy of doctrinal orthodoxy is feminist and womanist theologians. Mary Daly, Rosemary R. Ruether, Carter Heyward, Rebecca Chopp, Delores Williams, and Jacquelyn Grant are some of the leading figures in this movement.[34] These theologians would define orthopraxis as that praxis which affirms and enhances the humanity of women and liberates them from the chains of gender discrimination and oppression. While each of these theologians has her own particular emphases and specific perspectives, they all belong to the overall movement for the liberation of women. Feminist theologians bring to the discussion a combination of class and gender issues, whereas womanist theologians argue for a combination of the class, gender, and race issues in the discussion of liberation.

Theologians from those parts of the world where communities and societies are marked by a combination of poverty and religious pluralism see orthopraxis as that praxis which addresses the problem of poverty without losing sight of the dialogue between people of such differing religious traditions as Hinduism, Buddhism, and Islam. For example, Stanley J. Samartha, an Indian Christian theologian, argues for a revised christology and demands that such a christology should "take into account both the Christian experience of interreligious dialogue and Christian involvement in the political and social struggle for justice in society."[35] Here again one can detect both an invitation to take the historical Jesus as the central point of reference, and a call to move from orthodoxy to orthopraxis, coupling issues of sociopolitical justice and liberation with concerns for interreligious peace and reconciliation.

The inadequacy of the traditional christologies I have described illustrates another connection between the local-contextual and the global in christology today. Anyone who engages in christological articulation today must take into account questions of oppression and liberation, recognizing the precedence of orthopraxis over orthodoxy. By using the concept of guru as a model, I will attempt a christology that takes these issues seriously and engages theologians from different parts of the world in a common dialogue and conversation.

INAPPROPRIATENESS OF ABSOLUTISTIC CLAIMS

From its inception orthodox christology has maintained that only in Christ can one find the unique revelation of God and the final salvation of humanity. This absolutistic claim has been seen, especially during the missionary era (from the seventeenth through much of the twentieth century C.E.), as quite appropriate, credible, and feasible. Today we live in a different world. The world of the late twentieth century has an entirely different sense of religious pluralism, one that has raised serious questions for christology. As Alan Race points out:

> To say that we live in a religiously plural world is not new. What is new, however, is the increasing awareness that this brings with it serious theological issues for the Christian church. . . . Is the presence of God to be found only within one community of faith? Or is [God] more chameleon-like than that, dancing through history, enticing men and women into faith irrespective of the cultural shape of their response? These are major questions which strike at the core of Christian conviction.[36]

Moreover, the increasing number of opportunities for conversation and dialogue between different religionists creates occasions for Christians to wonder about their exclusive claims with regard to Christ. When one begins to recognize a certain common ground between various religions and the seriousness and authenticity of the spirituality of the other, one is forced to ask, "Why Jesus of Nazareth, after all? What is so unique and final about him?"

This century has seen an intense debate on the question of the uniqueness and finality of Christ. Ernst Troeltsch was one of the pioneers in this questioning of the absolutistic claims of Christianity.[37] More recently, theologians such as John Hick, Paul Knitter, Stanley Samartha, and Wilfred C. Smith have challenged the traditional understanding of the uniqueness of Christ and have offered ways of reinterpreting these claims in light of the present situation of religious pluralism. *The Myth of Christian Uniqueness: Toward a Pluralistic Theology of Religions,* published in 1987, pushed this idea to the center of today's christological discussions.[38] A subsequent volume, which questioned some of the theses of the contributors to the first, followed.[39] More recently, evangelical theologians have been in conversation with one another over this issue.[40]

The theological and christological issues involved in this discussion are quite complex and manifold. If one takes into serious account the emerging historical consciousness that asserts a relativistic understanding of religious beliefs, one may either have to abandon completely the idea of the finality of Christ or affirm this uniqueness and finality *only* in relation to the communities that adhere to the Christian faith. From this perspective, it is appropriate (and manageable) to say that Christ is unique and final *for Christians*. On the other hand one may expand the idea of Christ to such an extent that all human approximation to salvation and fulfillment is included in the idea "Christ." Whatever is good, beautiful, true, and salvific is so only through Christ. The two views that I have mentioned here are usually referred to as pluralism and inclusivism, while the claim that Christ is final and unique in a constitutive sense is called exclusivism. This threefold arrangement of exclusivism, inclusivism, and pluralism has helped in the initial stages of the discussion.[41] Yet we now find ourselves in a situation where these categories are no longer helpful; we need to press on to other ways of talking about the uniqueness and finality of Christ.

Here we find yet another point of contact between the local and the global in christological articulation. The idea of the uniqueness and finality of Christ in its absolutistic form is a problem for Christians all over the world, one with which Asian, African, and other two-thirds world theologians all grapple. Similarly, with the arrival of larger and larger numbers of immigrants from religious traditions other than Christianity, people in the West also are faced with this question. Hindu thinkers too are troubled by the absolutistic claims of christology and have invited Christians to engage in a reformulation of the idea of the uniqueness of Christ. Therefore, by employing the Hindu concept of guru as a christological model, I attempt to enable both a discussion and a reformulation of the uniqueness of Christ at a point where the local and the global intersect.

What I have outlined so far are some of the reasons for engaging in a bilingual or cross-cultural christology. My own personal history and the christological debates that have gone on in recent years point clearly to the need for a cross-cultural christology. Using the concept of guru as found in one of the Hindu traditions, I attempt in this book one such christology. Chapter 2 introduces the reader to the particular Hindu theological tradition at which we will be looking, namely, Saiva Siddhanta, and the concept of guru found within that tradition. As a means of discovering some directions for our own work, the next chapter examines the ways in which theologians have (and have not) employed the idea of guru in their christological articulation. Chapter 4 paints an imaginative picture of Jesus, the guru, giving the reader a glimpse of what Jesus the Christ might look like when one uses the concept of guru as a christological model. Chapter 5 evaluates this picture, delineating the possibilities and problems in such a christology. This evaluation leads to a discussion of methodological issues and the criteria for a cross-cultural christology in the final chapter.

Before we embark on this christology, let us remind ourselves again that christology is a dialogue. Robert Berkey makes the point well:

> Christology is never final but always in dialogue: with the early church, with the religious and mythological presuppositions and commitments of the Jewish and Hellenistic world, and perhaps most important, with the worldviews of our own age and time . . . Christologies, be they ancient or modern, are evoked first and always by dialogue.[42]

CHAPTER 2

THE CONCEPT OF GURU
IN SAIVA SIDDHANTA

The Saiva Siddhanta philosophy of Tamilnadu is one of the most reflective and systematic schools of Hinduism in India today, the significance of which has been acknowledged by Western and Indian scholars. For example, in 1900, G. U. Pope, an English missionary who pioneered the metrical translation of Saivite hymns into English, wrote that

> the Caiva Siddhanta system is the most elaborate, influential, and undoubtedly the most intrinsically valuable of all the religions of India. It is peculiarly the South Indian, and Tamil, religion; and must be studied by everyone who hopes to understand and influence the great South-Indian peoples.[1]

Saivite scholars today as well claim Saiva Siddhanta to be "the choicest product of the Dravidian intellect."[2]

"Siddhanta" is a compound word, made up of the Sanskrit terms "siddha" and "anta." The first word means "established" or "admitted to be true or right," while the second means "end" or "conclusion." Together they denote "established end, final end . . . settled opinion or doctrine."[3] John H. Piet, in his well-acclaimed book on Saiva Siddhanta, provides this concise definition:

> The Saiva Siddhanta, in other words, means the conclusion of conclusions—that which speaks the last religious-philosophical word. It is the final authority, the terminus of philosophical thought, the capstone of religious belief. By its very name, it claims that nothing higher exists.[4]

"Saiva" refers to those Hindus or the Hindu schools who use the name "Siva" for the Ultimate Being or God. Therefore, "Saiva Siddhanta" means the established philosophy of the worshipers of Siva. However, Siva-worshipers themselves belong to several sects, which differ from one another on matters of particular doctrines and practices. Saiva Siddhanta, then, can refer to virtually all the Saivite sects and their philosophies. But traditionally the term has come to designate the religious and philosophical thought of the Saivites in Tamilnadu, with special reference to the writings known as *Meykanta Sattiram* ("the treatises that have seen the truth"). I use the term "Saiva Siddhanta" as a synonym for Tamil Saivism.

HISTORY OF SAIVA SIDDHANTA

The origin of Saivism in India is not easily traceable, since the historical evidences are few and unreliable. Those who attribute the beginnings of Saivism to the period before the coming of the Aryans base their arguments on archaeological findings at Mohenjo-daro and Harappa in the northwestern part of India. They would date the origin of Saivism at 2000 B.C.E. or earlier. As Nilakanta Sastri, a leading Indian historian, writes:

> The origins of Saivism are lost in obscurity, but clearly the Saivism of history is a blend of two lines of development, the Aryan or Vedic and the pre-Aryan. . . . It is not a single cult but a federation of allied cults.[5]

As far as Tamil Saivism is concerned, these two lines of development are not merely two religious philosophies or cults but rather two separate ethnic (Aryan and Dravidian), cultural (North Indian and South Indian), and linguistic (Sanskrit and Tamil) traditions. Moreover, Sastri is quite right in designating Saivism as "a federation of allied cults," because varied understandings of Siva have merged in Saivism. In Siva we see "the impersonation of the dissolving and disintegrating powers and processes of nature," "the eternal reproductive power of Nature," "the great typical ascetic and self-mortifier," "the contemplative philosopher and learned sage," "a wild and jovial mountaineer," and finally "a being half-male and half-female."[6] This is true as well of the vision of Siva one finds in Tamil Saivism. One cannot easily separate the Vedic and Dravidian elements in Saivism; one should rather view Tamil Saivism as the Tamil version of the composite Saivite tradition.

The earliest extant body of literature in Tamil is known as *Sangam* literature.[7] Most scholars would agree that it belongs to the period roughly from 250 B.C.E. to 250 C.E. Though these writings refer to such mythological descriptions of Siva as "the Lord with the blue throat" and "the God under the banyan tree" and so on, the name "Siva" never appears in them.[8] Some of the great epics that were written following the Sangam period do contain references to Siva and Saivite faith.[9] The two significant didactic works of this period are *Tirukkural* and *Naladiyar.* Whereas *Naladiyar* is, beyond doubt, the work of a Jain poet, the religious persuasion of the author of *Tirukkural* is much debated. Some consider it a Saivite work, and several Saivite thinkers of the later centuries do quote *Tirukkural* freely in their expositions of Saiva Siddhanta.[10] Whether the author of *Tirukkural* was a Saivite or not, the later Saivites did see him as their religious ally.

Tirumantiram, written during the period 300–600 C.E., is the first and most fully developed Tamil work on Saiva Siddhanta, and thus it becomes the basis for all the later writings. The word "Siddhanta" appears for the first time in *Tirumantiram:* "Since the soul attains salvation in Siddhanta, the devotees of Siddhanta became Jivan-Muktas; as Siddhanta is the quintessence of all the Vedas, it is the right path that will discover Siva."[11] *Tirumantiram* is the first Saivite writing that depreciates the differences between the Vedas (the earliest scriptures, compiled around 1500 B.C.E.) and the Agamas (a post-Vedic set of scriptures), and thus incorporates the Agamic truths as an essential and formative part of the Tamil Saivite tradition. This work marks the beginnings of a distinctive Saivite tradition, later to be designated Saiva Siddhanta.

The seventh century C.E. began a new chapter in the history of Tamil Saivism. A band of bhakti poets, known as *nayanmars,* emerged between the seventh century and the tenth. The most important of these poets were Appar, Campantar, Cuntarar, and Manikkavacakar. Claiming to have had genuine encounters with the divine in one form or another, they were motivated by a great "evangelistic" fervor to pass on to others their own experience of devotion to Siva.

The existing brahmanical form of Hinduism was not adequate to meet the challenge posed by Jainism and Buddhism. It was not the religion of the common people, and Sanskrit was the only language it employed in religious discourse. It also maintained the caste system rigidly and could not stand up to the Jain and Buddhist call for a more egalitarian society. Only the bhakti poets, with their inspiring hymns in Tamil and their opposition to caste hierarchy, were able to meet the challenges of these rival religious systems.

One can easily detect a sense of Tamil nationalism in the writings of these poets. Siva is often portrayed as the God of the Tamils and as a great patron of Tamil literature and music. For example, Manikkavacakar praises Siva as "Civan, Lord of the Southern Land."[12] The hymns of these poets were collected by Nanbi-andar-nambi at the beginning of the eleventh century into *Panniru Tirumurai* (the twelve sacred writings).[13]

The period from the twelfth to the fourteenth century saw the rise of a Saivite literature that can be classified as philosophical or theological. These writings, fourteen in number, form a single corpus called *Meykanta Sattiram*.[14] This collection was the result of an attempt to systematize and bring into a coherent whole the history and doctrine of Tamil Saivism up to that time. It was a philosophical enterprise in tune with the mood of the day—the composition of similar philosophical writings was taking place at the same time in Vaishnavism. Up to the beginning of the fourteenth century, the Tamil region was ruled by such Tamil kings as the Pallavas, the Cholas, the Pandyas, and the Cheras, most of whom were great patrons of Saivism. The fourteenth century saw the rising power of the Vijayanagar empire, to be followed by Muslim rule for the next two centuries. By the nineteenth century India was completely under the rule of the British, and, due to the work of its missionaries, Christianity became a recognizable, and in some ways influential, reality in Tamilnadu. By this time Saivism possessed a rich past and was a clearly defined school of religious thought with its own hymns, hagiography, theology, and mythologies.

The history of Saiva Siddhanta during the modern period holds two notable features. The first is the rise of two important Saivite poets: Tayumanavar (latter part of the eighteenth century) and Ramalinga Adigal (1823–1874). Both of these individuals moved toward a more catholic or ecumenical view of God and Saiva religion as a whole. Second, a clear revival of Saiva Siddhanta has taken place during the last 100 years because of the work of the various Saiva monasteries *(matam)* and the Saiva Siddhanta Works Publishing Society of Madras and Tirunelveli. Saivite scholars such as J. M. Nallaswami Pillai translated the Siddhanta texts into English and made them available to Western scholars. The publication of a translation of *Sivananapotam* by H. R. Hoisington in 1895 and a translation of *Tiruvacakam* by G. U. Pope in 1900 furthered the cause of Tamil Saivism among English-speaking scholars. In 1944 the Sri Arulnandi Sivacharya Swamigal Sivagnana Siddhiyar Lectureship Endowment was instituted at the Annamalai University, Chidambaram, for a yearly series of lectures on Saiva Siddhanta to be delivered at the Benares Hindu University and Allahabad University.[15] These lectures brought an all-India character to Tamil Saivism. The International Institute of Saiva Siddhanta Research at Dharmapuram Adhinam, together with Saivite leaders and scholars in Malaysia, has been hosting a series of international seminars on Saiva Siddhanta since the early 1980s. The Madurai-Kamaraj University at Madurai, which was founded nearly three decades ago, has a separate department of Saiva Siddhanta, where a regular program of graduate-level research in Saiva Siddhanta is in place.

This brief survey of the history of Saiva Siddhanta clearly demonstrates that Saiva Siddhanta has been one of the leading components of Tamil religious thought over the centuries. It has come under varied influences from several other religious traditions and changing political climates. From its beginnings in local village cults to its highly reflective and speculative tradition in the fourteenth century C.E. and on into the present, Saivism has maintained its Tamil character.

If such is the dominance of Saivite thought within the religious life of Tamilnadu, anyone who constructs a christology that is to be relevant and meaningful to the people of Tamilnadu should take Saiva Siddhanta into serious account. The concept of guru in Saiva Siddhanta, as we shall see later, is most helpful to the construction of such a relevant christology. Furthermore, a christology constructed in the context of Saiva Siddhanta can and does offer fresh insights into the person and work of Christ, along with several methodological challenges. These insights and challenges can be particularly relevant and fruitful for christological reflection in other parts of the world, a fact we will explore more fully later.

THE CENTRAL THEMES OF SAIVA SIDDHANTA

One of the best ways to explicate the central theological ideas of Saiva Siddhanta is to examine the three underlying categories that govern the system. These are the Sanskrit terms *pati* (God), *pasu* (soul), and *pasam* (bondage). Present-day Saivites largely use the Tamil equivalents *irai, uyir,* and *talai.* Both *Tirumantiram* and *Sivananapotam* use the same three categories to organize their reflective presentation of Saiva Siddhanta. This threefold scheme is quite appropriate for examining the concept of guru in Saiva Siddhanta because the idea of guru is largely shaped by presuppositions concerning God, soul, and bondage. Let me begin with the concept of God.

The Concept of God

Saiva Siddhanta, true to its name, treats Siva as the Supreme Being. Siva, together with Brahma and Vishnu, is also one of the *tirumurti,* the three chief gods of the Hindu pantheon. As far as Saiva Siddhanta is concerned, Siva is the ultimate reality above whom there is none. To avoid, I believe, confusing this Siva with the Siva of the Hindu pantheon, the Saivites sometimes use the word "Sivam" to denote God, the ultimate reality. Whereas "Siva" (or "Sivan") possesses a personal and masculine ending, the word "Sivam" has a neuter ending. So by using "Sivam" one can refer to "Sivahood" in the sense of Godhead or divinity, rather than to an individual, masculine god called Siva. The following poem from *Tirumantiram* illustrates the use of "Sivam" for God.

> The ignorant think that love (anpu) and God (civam) [or Sivam] are two
> (different things); they do not know that love is God. After knowing
> that love
> is God, they remain possessed of love which is God.[16]

Even today the most popular motto among the Saivites is *anpe Sivam* (love is God). Sivam is also referred to as *pati* (lord), *pasupati* (lord of cattle), and *haran* (destroyer).

The use of the word "Sivam" for God helps the Saivites to differentiate God from the different forms of God, and thus avoid polytheistic overtones. For example, while discussing the concept of God, S. Gangadharan, a Saivite scholar, has this to say:

> The self-existent Sivam is the divine ground whose essence may be described as unconditioned Being, independent consciousness and infinite, i.e., unlimited bliss. This is Sivam or *Tarcivam* which has no modifications and this is the essential definition of God.[17]

Therefore, it is quite legitimate to make consistent use of "Sivam" for God when discussing Saiva Siddhanta. Moreover, the use of the word "Sivam" enables one to avoid sexist language for God. Though the Saivites quite often use the masculine or neuter pronoun for Sivam, their intent is not to promote sexist understandings of God.[18] Therefore, I use the word "Sivam" instead of "Siva" throughout, except in places where the male Siva is implied. Every now and then I also use the English word "God" interchangeably with "Sivam," a practice the Saivites also employ when they write about their faith in English.

Sivam is the creator of this universe. Sivam is the efficient cause of the universe, while energy or power *(sakti)* is the instrumental cause, and *maya* (matter) is the material cause. *Maya*, in Saiva Siddhanta, does not mean "illusion" or "non-real" (as is the case elsewhere in Hindu thought), but rather denotes the matter that has been used by God in the process of creation. The purpose of creation is to give space and time for souls to work out their salvation, and consequently be cleansed of the impurities that bind them. Thus God's creative activity is itself an act of God's grace. A poem in *Sivananacittiyar*, one of the philosophical works, expresses this idea:

> If you ask why God should exercise these powers, we may reply that this is His mere play. We may also point out that by these acts of Grace,

He makes the souls eat the fruit of their Karma and thus get rid of their Mala and attain Mukti.[19]

If Sivam is the Creator, then for the Saivites, Sivam is apart from the creation. God is a transcendent being who cannot be identified with any of the things or persons of this world. In *Sivananacittiyar* we read:

> He [Sivam] is not one of those objects which are subject to bonds and are not free. He has neither beginning nor end. He is infinite. As such it cannot be postulated that my Supreme Father is only this or that, and that He cannot become this or that; and therefore any such postulate regarding the nature of the Supreme does not admit any refutation either.[20]

The same kind of sentiment is expressed in this poem from *Tevaram*:

> One cannot write and show that
> this one,
> this kind,
> of this shape,
> of this color
> God is . . .[21]

This emphasis on the otherness of Sivam does not imply an unbridgeable gap between Sivam and the created order. Sivam does pervade all and can assume forms to be accessible to the creatures. In *Sivananacittiyar* we read:

> If He did not, out of His Supreme Grace, assume forms, there would be nobody who could give out Vedas and Agamas, and there would be nobody who could impart instruction, in the form of the Guru to the Gods, men, and the residents of nether region and so nobody can secure salvation.[22]

The idea of Sivam's assuming forms in no way contradicts the transcendent character of Sivam. Nor does it imply the concept of *avatar* or incarnation. The *avatar* concept is built on the idea that the incarnate God goes through the processes of birth, growth, and death. Since God is transcendent and apart from creation, God cannot and will not join Godself to matter and the material processes.

The overriding motif in the concept of God in Saiva Siddhanta is divine grace. The two words that are used most often in this connection are *anpu* (love) and *arul* (grace or unconditional giving). Sivam is considered to have five functions: creation, conservation, destruction, obscuration, and granting of grace. Though the granting of grace appears as a separate function in this list, the Saivites consider all five functions as expressions of divine grace:

> Destruction is to give rest to the souls; Creation is to enable the souls to indulge in karma; Conservation is to help souls to be attracted to karma; Obscuration is intended to bring out equanimity towards pain and pleasure; Granting of Grace is to free the souls from bondage; If one looks closely, all the five functions are themselves grace. So refrain from complaining![23]

In all these discussions we notice that the graciousness of Sivam is understood in relation to the souls. God's grace is to help souls free themselves from their bondage; hence it is always a saving grace. Because of this repeated emphasis on the graciousness of Sivam, Sivam emerges primarily as a gracious savior, even though the philosophical writings begin with the idea of Sivam as creator. Sivam is the creator, sustainer, or destroyer, all because Sivam is the savior.

The Concept of Soul

The second eternal category in Saiva Siddhanta is that of *pasu* or *uyir*. *Pasu* means "cattle" or "cow." The soul is *pasu* because in the Vedic tradition Sivam is known as the lord of the cattle *(pasupati)*. *Uyir* means "life" or "that which makes a being a living being." The word *anma*, which is derived from the Sanskrit term *atman*, also is used in the Saivite literature to denote the soul.

Sutram 3 of *Sivananapotam* attempts to prove the existence of the soul:

> There is a soul which exists separate from the body and from the instruments of the body, for the following reasons: 1. There is some-

thing which is able to say "No" (to the proposition that there is a soul). 2. There is something which is able to say "My body." 3. There is something which knows the five senses. 4. There is something which knows dreams. 5. There is something which knows in the state of sleep when the body does not eat or work. 6. There is something which is able to know when taught.[24]

The main thrust of the argument here is to say that the soul is qualitatively different from the body. It is eternal and nonmaterial. If the soul is the subject and the world the object of its experiences, then the body is the soul's instrument in experiencing the world. Whereas the soul is not dependent on the body, the body is fully dependent on the soul for its life, activity, and knowledge. The relationship between the soul and the inner organs of the human body is like the relation between a king and his ministers.

Souls are classified into different stages or *avasthas*. A poem in *Sivananacittiyar* explains the point thus:

> The causal or subtle Avastha are three, called Kevala, Sakala and Suddha. The soul is in Kevala when the soul is by itself (without volition etc.). It is in Sakala, when God unites it to all its senses and organs. It is in Suddha, when leaving birth, it is free from all *mala*.[25]

It is the *sakala* state that is relevant to us because that is the state in which God unites the soul to a body. In the *sakala* state the human individual is viewed as a universe in miniature, with thirty-six *tattuvams* (principles or properties). *Unmai Vilakkam*, one of the books in *Meykanta Sattiram*, describes these thirty-six *tattuvams* in detail. At a much later period, two treatises called *Tattuvapirakasam* and *Tattuvakkattalai* were written mainly to explain the thirty-six properties of the human being. These include such things as the five elements (earth, water, fire, air, and ether), the five senses, and the affective and inner organs.

Two things become clear in all these discussions: first, souls are many; and second, the soul is distinct from the body. To this we should add the view that the soul, though eternal, is distinct from God. The word *advaita* (nondual) is used in Saiva Siddhanta to explain the relation between the soul and God. In this context *advaita* means something very different from its meaning within the monistic schools of Hindu philosophy. As Piet puts it,

> For the Siddhantin, therefore, the word "advaita" denotes the relationship that exists between the soul and God. . . . It is not a relationship similar to that between gold and ornaments made from the gold, which are materially one but formally different, nor to that between light and darkness, which are mutually exclusive. Rather, it is the relationship of two things which in their union are neither one nor two nor neither.[26]

This relation between the soul and God is an eternal one. Though eternal, it does not include final bliss or complete happiness, because the soul is also in a predicament; namely, it is in bondage.

The Concept of Bondage

Pasam literally means "a snare, trap, noose, tie, bond, cord, chain, fetter."[27] The Tamil equivalent of this term is *talai*. The Saivites believe that the soul is not able to enjoy bliss and union with Sivam because it is in bondage. This bondage is composed of three *malas* (impurities), namely, *anavam* (egocentricity), *karma* (action-result complex), and *maya* (matter).[28] The soul, which is infinite and all-pervading, because of its association with these three impurities becomes finite, limited, and ignorant.

Anavam is known as the original impurity *(sahaja malam)*. It is a beginningless entity that attaches itself to the soul from eternity, blinds the vision of the soul, and dupes it into thinking that *anavam* does not exist. Therefore, it is called the impurity of darkness *(irul malam)*.[29] This deluding character of *anavam* or ignorance lies at the root of the human predicament. The fundamental problem of the soul is thus that it lacks knowledge.

The second impurity is *karma,* namely action and its results. *Karma* is made up of both good and bad actions, which result in a cycle of births and deaths for the soul.[30] It should be noted, however, that the cycle of births does not automatically follow *karma* nor does *karma* by itself effect rebirth. It is Sivam who imputes the results to the actions in the form of different births, like a king who metes out reward and punishment to his subjects.[31]

The third impurity is *maya*. *Maya* does not mean "illusion"; rather, it is the primordial matter that is shaped by Sivam into created order. *Maya* gives to the soul the location, the instruments, and the objects of experience. Saiva Siddhanta classifies *maya* into several categories, the full number of which need not occupy our attention here. Suffice it to say that at the heart of the human problem resides the fact that the soul identifies itself with the instruments and objects of experience and is ignorant of its transcendental character and its relation to God.

The preceding examination of three central categories of Saiva Siddhanta, namely, *pati, pasu,* and *pasam,* has given us a picture of the savior (Sivam), the saved (the soul), and the need for salvation (bondage). We need as well to look at the process by which freedom from bondage is effected. This process possesses four salient features: First, salvation is not a static event but a work in progress. Both *Meykanta Sattiram* and *Tattuvakkattalai* refer to the various stages through which the soul must travel before it reaches the feet of Sivam, that is, before it attains final bliss.[32] Second, the tradition repeatedly emphasizes the total inability of the soul to save itself by its own efforts. It is Sivam and Sivam alone who can save souls from their bondage.[33] Third, souls are of different kinds according to the intensity of their bondage. The first group of souls is called *vinnanakalar,* that is, those who have only one impurity, namely, *anavam.* These are souls that are not yet connected to a body. The second group is *piralayakalar,* those who have two impurities, *anavam* and *karma.* These are souls who belong to the period of destruction or deluge and are not yet united with *maya.* The third group, called *sakalar,* includes all living human beings who are bound by all the three impurities. To each of these groups Sivam has a distinctive way of granting salvation. Finally, the primary emphasis is on the salvation of *souls* and not on that of humans, other creatures, or the world. The world and worldly existence are simply the instruments or the working ground for souls to attain salvation. They are not the objects of God's salvific activity. The two foci of salvation are thus God and souls. It is in the context of this vision of salvation that the concept of guru is to be located and understood.

THE CONCEPT OF GURU IN SAIVA SIDDHANTA

"Guru" is a Sanskrit term and is transliterated in most of the Indian languages. As suggested by Joel D. Mlecko, it has three layers of meaning.[34] The first layer has to do with the idea of the guru as the dispeller of ignorance. The second is that the guru is powerful and holy. The third is that the guru is one who is called by God. After discussing these three layers of meaning, Mlecko summarizes in this way:

> In a word, the guru is indispensable for spiritual development. In early Hinduism he was a vital factor in imparting Vedic knowledge; in later thought the guru became the visible embodiment of truth and in some cases he was worshipped as an incarnate deity.[35]

Saiva Siddhanta uses several other terms to talk about the spiritual teacher. *Acariyan,* one such term,[36] is derived from the Sanskrit word *acarya,* meaning a spiritual guide or teacher who knows and teaches the *acara* or rules of initiation and conduct.[37] Given the fact that there is an elaborate system of *diksa* (initiation process) in Saiva Siddhanta, this term is most likely to refer to an *acarya* who initiates a disciple into a religious order or experience. Other terms that are used include *ariyan* or *antanan* (honorable man or sage), and *natan* or *aran* (lord).

The concept of guru, as such, is not peculiar to Saiva Siddhanta; it is common to most of the religious traditions of India.[38] The following are some of the features common to the understanding of the term "guru" in all of these traditions. First, the word "guru" denotes a human being, male or female. A guru is fully human; his or her humanity is never doubted or denied. Even the individual guru movements, which never hesitate simply and straightforwardly to equate their guru with God, would not deny the guru's humanity. Second, a guru is always understood in relation to God. Somehow the guru represents God, or God is seen to act through the guru. Some may consider the guru as an incarnation of God. Others may view the guru as symbolizing the presence of God. Therefore, the concept of guru is always theological. Third, the idea of guru is invariably linked with the process of salvation, and hence it is also soteriological. On the basis of these common features we can say that the guru is a human being who has reached a higher level in the process of salvation and whose significance is to be understood, both theologically (i.e., in relation to God) and soteriologically (i.e., in relation to the attainment of salvation), as one who assists other humans to reach final release.

Yet there are certain features of the concept of guru which are peculiar to Saiva Siddhanta. These may be grouped under three headings: hymnic discourse, philosophical discourse, and narrative discourse. These three modes of discourse exhibit a wide range of variety, both stylistically and chronologically, and each deserves careful and separate attention. However, I limit my attention to those passages and poems that have a direct bearing on the explication of the guru concept, though not necessarily to those where the word "guru" appears. As just noted, such other terms as *acariyan, ariyan, antanan,* and *aiyan* are also used to denote guru, so passages where these terms appear will also be considered.

Hymnic Discourse

The material we consider in this section is traditionally known as *Tirumurai,* the holy writings. These are hymns that are set for a context of worship, and as such they express the individual's devotion (bhakti) to Lord Siva. *Tirumantiram, Tevaram,* and *Tiruvacakam* are the three books among the twelve in the *Tirumurai* that explicitly deal with the guru concept and its related ideas.

1) *Tirumantiram* mentions clearly that freedom from *pasam* (bondage) is possible only through a guru. Saivism is referred to as *guruneri* (the way of the guru).[39] For example, we read:

> Illumination is beholding the guru's sacred form.
> Illumination is chanting the guru's sacred name.
> Illumination is hearing the guru's sacred word.
> Illumination is pondering the guru's sacred image.[40]

The word that is used to denote salvation is *telivu,* which means "illumination" or "making something clear." *Telivu* is possible only through seeing, hearing, and meditating on the guru. This poem sets the tone for the treatment of the concept of guru in the whole of *Tirumantiram.* In all the references to guru in *Tirumantiram,* one can easily detect the emphasis on what the guru does rather than on who the guru is. The guru's touch helps one to free oneself from the clutches of repeated births.[41] The guru shows what is *sat, asat,* and *satasat* (real, unreal, and real-unreal) by placing the guru's feet on the head and heart of the disciple.[42] One can give several more examples from *Tirumantiram* to illustrate the idea that the basic functions of the guru are to remove the impurities that bind the soul and to help the soul escape the cycle of births. These functions are carried on by the guru's look, the guru's words, or the guru's very appearance. The disciple appropriates them by listening, chanting, meditating upon, and worshiping the guru, because the guru is Sivam in human form.

Tirumantiram mentions the three preliminary stages through which the soul travels to arrive at a position to recognize the guru. Poem 2262 refers to these three stages as *iruvinaioppu, malaparipakam,* and *sattinipatam.*[43] These stages, though not discussed in detail in *Tirumantiram,* do receive elaboration in the later philosophical writings. In another poem (1527), Tirumular, the author of *Tirumantiram,* sees the descent of the saving power of God's grace as coinciding with the coming of the guru. He says that the *arulsatti* comes as guru—*innarul satti guruvena vantu.*[44] *Arulsatti* can be interpreted as one of the five functions of Sivam, such as creation, preservation, obscuration, destruction, and the granting of grace. In that case Sivam does not come as a guru, but rather the gracious function of Sivam takes a human form in the guru. Interestingly, in the later philosophical writings the theological difficulty involved in reconciling God's transcendent and formless character with God's assumption of a human form is resolved by appealing to the idea that it is God's grace that embodies itself in a human being, the guru.

2) *Tevaram,* as a collection of hymns addressed to Sivam, does use the title "guru" to refer to Sivam, along with a multitude of other titles. Appar sings, *gurvane atiyenai kurikkole* (O! Guru! Take possession of your servant!)[45] Cuntarar sings, *Kuriye, ennutaiya gurve un kurreval ceyven* (My Goal! My guru! I shall be thy lowly servant!).[46] In none of these references in *Tevaram* is there an explicit reference to the human appearance of Sivam. Rather, Sivam is often portrayed as acting in the hearts of the disciples. For example, Appar sings, *matanencam manampukum guruvinai* (the guru who enters

my mind and my foolish heart).[47] Both the breadth and the variety of Sivam's appearances and the interiority of the salvific activity of Sivam make the guru concept function in broader terms; it is not restricted to the appearance of Sivam in human form.

3) Manikkavacakar, in his *Tiruvacakam,* refers to the idea of guru in three distinct ways.[48] First, guru is connected with particular shrines. For example, he speaks of "Guru-pearl that rules in Gogari,"[49] and "Guru-pearl in Kudal shining bright."[50] In these references one can say that Sivam is guru. Second, some of the references speak of the guru as the human appearance of Sivam. For example,

> The One most precious Infinite to earth came down;
> Nor did I greatness of the Sage Supreme contemn
> Who came in grace. (4, 75ff.)

> Thee Endless One, benignly manifest, diffusing light
> —as Man—I saw thee come. (18, 14)

Third, the idea of *atkollal* (taking possession) emphasizes the inward activity of the guru. For example there are such statements as *kattatkollum gurumaniye* (Guru-gem who guarding makest me Thine!) (50, 13; 25, 10). Manikkavacakar describes the saving activity of Sivam in terms of God's taking possession of him and making him God's own. Glenn Yocum writes:

> A sisya [disciple] is supposed to surrender himself completely to his guru. The guru "indwells" his disciple. In effect, the sisya negates himself. He lives only for his guru. As can readily be inferred, there is some overlap between this attitude and that of possession by a god.[51]

Here again, Sivam is guru, but this time an interior guru who takes possession of the soul.

To sum up, I make the following observations. *Tirumantiram* outlines the main elements in the concept of guru, which are to be elaborated in detail in the later philosophical writings. The absolute need for a guru if one is to attain release, the idea of guru functioning as God to the disciple, and the vision of guru as one who initiates the disciple into the salvation process are all found in *Tirumantiram.*

Tevaram and *Tiruvacakam* also employ the idea of guru. However, the peculiar significance of the concept of guru is lost in the multitude of titles that are ascribed to Sivam in these two texts. *Tiruvacakam* uses the guru concept to signify the human appearance of Sivam; yet one cannot be sure whether it refers to the physical presence of the guru or to a spiritual indwelling of the guru in the hearts of the disciples.

Philosophical Discourse

Now let us go on to look at the philosophical writings known as the *Meykanta Sattiram*.[52] Each of the fourteen books that belong to this corpus is accompanied by several commentaries. Therefore, when one analyzes the concept of guru in these writings, one must also take the commentaries into serious consideration. I will not attempt a book-by-book examination here, but rather will highlight four dominant themes under which the concept of guru appears in these writings.

SIVAM IN THE FORM OF A GURU   The eighth sutra of *Sivananapotam* uses the following metaphor to describe the predicament of the soul, as well as its release from bondage through the appearance of Sivam as guru.[53] A prince who happens to grow up among hunters in the forest does not know that he is the king's son. The king comes in search of his son, reveals to him his true identity, and takes him back to the palace, which is his rightful place. Likewise the soul does not know its true identity and its relationship to Sivam, having identified itself with the hunters, namely, the five senses. Sivam comes in the form of a guru and helps the soul to realize its true identity and unites the soul to Sivaself in a relationship of love. What does it mean to say that Sivam comes in the form of a guru? How does one reconcile this with the fact that Sivam is the Supreme Lord and Creator who is utterly apart from the created order? Sivam is formless, immutable, and belongs to the world beyond the phenomenal world. If so, how could Sivam assume a human form? Is such a guru a human being in appearance only? Or if one accepts the full humanity of the guru, what does it mean to say that Sivam comes in the form of a guru?

These are questions that the Saivite philosophers themselves raise and attempt to answer. For example, *Vinavenpa,* poem 8, reads thus:

> If the Lord is formless, he cannot be with form. If he has a form, then he cannot be formless. A thing cannot have two opposing natures. If so, how is it that the Lord is seen in a form and that he is wearing a body? O! Sampanta of the great *Kadantai!* Tell me![54]

These questions are answered in several different ways. The commentator of *Vinavenpa,* discussing this poem, sees the formless as the cause *(karanam)* and the form as the effect *(kariyam).* He says that since Sivam is the cause behind everything, Sivam comes as a guru by Sivam's own causal power and sovereignty. It is an act of grace and is thus not easily explainable.[55] In all these attempts, the question concerning the person of the guru is bypassed by appealing to the sovereign power of Sivam and the mysterious character of Sivam's salvific activity. In other words, theological considerations overrule problematic concerns regarding the *person* of the guru.

Another way to face these questions is to appeal to soteriological considerations. Souls are classified under three groups—*vinnanakalar, piralayakalar,* and *sakalar.*[56] *Sakalars* (the living human beings) can reach knowledge only through their sensory perception. This means that Sivam needs to appear to them in a human form and effect salvation. The metaphor of salt and saltiness is used to explain this fact.[57] One cannot taste saltiness apart from concrete salt. Sivam, like saltiness, is formless. But to help us come to knowledge, Sivam takes a concrete form. The human appearance of Sivam is also seen as a way by which Sivam tricks souls into coming under Sivam's sway, just as a decoy is used to catch wild animals.[58] The two soteriological necessities these reflections encapsulate are (1) that only Sivam can save souls and (2) that souls can recognize and appropriate salvation only through a human being.[59] These two necessities justify God's coming as a guru. The person of the guru is understood in purely functional terms.

One should note at this point that Saiva Siddhanta rejects the idea of *avatar,* which is generally translated as "incarnation." *Avatar* literally means "descent." Saivism rejects the concept of *avatar* mainly because this concept assumes that the one who descends is born as a child, grows, and dies. This threefold process is something that belongs to the material and phenomenal world. Sivam cannot and will not go through such a process since Sivam is formless and immutable. This rejection of the concept of *avatar* means that Saiva Siddhanta has to use several metaphors to explain God's coming as a guru. The phrase that occurs most often is *manutac cattai catti* ("wearing the garment of humanity"). Another such phrase is *tiru-meni kontu vanta civan* ("Siva who came with a holy body"). The idea here is that, though Sivam is active in every soul as an inner being, it is the utter transparency of the guru to Sivam that makes the disciple see the guru as the very Sivam. This is so because the guru is one who has reached a higher stage of maturity in the salvation process.[60]

Mention should be made here of another phrase that is used to explain the human appearance of Sivam, namely, *eluntaruli* ("graciously rising").[61] Sivam graciously rises as a guru and effects liberation. In the person of the human guru, Sivam rises as the savior and frees the soul from bondage. This language is opposed to the *avatar* language that talks of God as coming down from above.

The language of embodiment also is used, whereby the guru is the embodiment of divine grace; it is God's grace or *arulsatti* that takes flesh in the guru. Of course God's grace is always present in the devotee. But now it is awakened and appears in a concrete form as guru. This seems to solve the problem of how the formless one could take form as a guru. It is not Sivam in Sivaself but Sivam's grace that is now seen in the guru.

The question regarding the person of the guru is answered, most interestingly, through the idea of first, second, and third persons in grammar.[62] To the *vinnanakalar,* Sivam appears in the first person as "I." This means that they can look inward within themselves and come to know Sivam. To the *piralayakalar* Sivam appears in the second person as "Thou," in the glorious divine form of a guru, as in a theophany. To the *sakalar,* Sivam appears in the third person as the "He" behind the "Thou." So when the disciple looks at the guru, outwardly the human guru is the "Thou" whom the disciple meets. But the "He" behind the "Thou" is Sivam. Sivam stands hidden behind the guru *(guruvativin maraintu ninru patarkkaiyanunarttap-pattu).* Here again the emphasis is on the functional aspect of the guru and not on an exploration of the nature of the guru in relation to Sivam. For all practical purposes this human is Sivam because it is Sivam who stands hidden behind him or her.

STAGES LEADING TO THE APPEARANCE OF THE GURU   According to Saiva Siddhanta, salvation is a long process, taking a soul through several births. This idea is expressed in many different ways. First, the idea of several *margas* (ways) and their respective goals signifies growth in the life of a soul. The four margas are *dasa marga* (the way of a servant), *putra marga* (the way of sonship), *saka marga* (the way of friendship), and *sanmarga* (the full way or the true way).[63] *Dasa marga* is the way in which a person serves Sivam like a servant by serving God's devotees and in Sivam's temples. This kind of service leads the soul to partial release, called *salokya* or living in the same world as Sivam. *Putra marga* is the way of devotion and of unceasingly praising Sivam as a true child of Sivam. This leads to the state of *samipya* in which the soul lives in nearness to Sivam. The third way, *sakamarga,* involves performing the various yogas and thus achieving *sarupya,* a state in which the soul is similar to Sivam. The final way, *sanmarga,* is the way in which the soul comes to true knowledge by studying the Vedas and the Agamas with the help of a guru. This leads to the state of complete release, which is called *sayujya* or union with Sivam. These four stages are also referred to by the terms *carya, kriya, yoga, and jnana.* The path of knowledge comes at the end and is the only way to perfect release. As Devasena-pati writes, "The emphasis all the time is on jnana, a feature common to the best Hindu thought. Carya, kriya etc. are considered preparatory stages, leading to but not constituting final release."[64] The appearance of the guru is the final stage in which the disciple is enabled to attain the knowledge that will lead one to liberation from bondage.

Second, there are references to another set of three stages that prepares the soul to recognize the guru as Sivam. These are *iruvinaioppu, malaparipakam,* and *sattinipatam. Iruvinaioppu* literally means "both actions similar"; that is, the soul comes to a stage in which good and bad, right and wrong, pain and pleasure are looked upon with equanimity. The soul reaches this stage through several austerities or *tapas,* which it performed in previous births. Equanimity is necessary for the appearance of the guru because as long as the soul is oscillating between good and bad, it will not be able to receive the knowledge that the guru offers.[65] Next comes *malaparipakam*. Once desire is relinquished, the *malas* (bondages) begin to meet the cause of their removal and are ready to be shed. Thus the stage of *malaparipakam* is an immediate consequence of *iruvinaioppu*. The soul has come to a restful state ready to receive instruction from a guru, and the *malas* have reached a ripened stage ready to fall off like a ripe fruit that falls from the tree. The third aspect of maturation is the divine preparation for the guru's appearance, called *sattini-patam*. This is the stage in which the power of grace descends and enables the appearance of the guru.

A third way to look at the salvation process is to locate it in the context of different religious traditions in India. *Sivananacittiyar* classifies religions as outer or inner, and locates Saiva Siddhanta as the innermost. When one is born as a Saiva Siddhanta, one can be sure that one has come to a stage of maturation. Then one goes again through the four stages of *carya, kriya, yoga,* and *jnana*, and finally reaches perfect release.

Fourth, one may classify the different stages as different kinds of knowledge. *Pasajnana*, the bondage-oriented knowledge, is in practical terms ignorance, in which the soul does not know itself or Sivam. The next stage is *pasujnana*, the soul-oriented knowledge. Here the soul is beginning to be aware of that which is behind the world of phenomena. But in discovering this, the soul identifies itself with Sivam and fails to see the sovereign distinctiveness of Sivam. The final stage is *patijnana*, the Lord-oriented knowledge, in which the soul knows both itself and its Lord in distinction and in the relationship of love and surrender.[66]

TITCAI, THE INITIATION PROCESS   *Titcai* or *tikkai* is derived from the Sanskrit word *diksa*, meaning "a preparation or consecration for a religious ceremony [or] initiation [or] any serious preparation."[67] *Titcai* is a combination of purificatory, catechetical, and initiatory processes. Saiva Siddhanta, as it is propounded in *Meykanta Satti-ram*, especially *Sivananacittiyar*, has an elaborate system of *titcai* through which the disciple must go once the disciple comes to recognize and surrender to the guru. The elaborate system of initiation requires the continuing physical presence of the guru. Here again the emphasis is on the guru's functioning as Sivam to the disciple rather than on Sivam's occasional appearance as guru.

GURU MARAPU OR SUCCESSION OF GURUS   The idea that the guru belongs to a succession of gurus starting from Sivam in heaven is present in *Sivapirakasam,* written by Umapati in 1306 C.E.[68] Umapati traces the succession of his own guru Maraijnanacampantar from Sivam through Meykantar and Arulnanti, the authors of *Sivananapotam* and *Sivananacittiyar* respectively. This idea of *guru marapu* is not a dominant one in the tradition, though the several monastic institutions *(matam)* are headed by gurus who come in a clearly defined succession of gurus.[69] This is confirmed by the fact that the Saivites do not indulge in mapping out genealogies of successive gurus, as do the Vaishnavites with their idea of *guruparamparai.* The lack of interest in *guru marapu* signals the open-ended character of the nature and function of the guru.

To sum up our examination of the guru concept in Saivite philosophical discourse, let me highlight the following aspects. The guru is both a teacher and an initiator. The guru's identity is defined neither by membership in a particular caste, nor by relation to a specific succession of gurus. It is rather the spiritual maturity of the guru that matters. Furthermore, the guru's humanity is never doubted or denied; yet at the same time the guru functions as God to the disciple. But the guru is neither God nor an *avatar* of God. It is the disciple who comes to recognize and imaginatively envision the guru to be functioning as God to him or her. This means that what the guru does for the disciple is far more important than what or who the guru is.

Narrative Discourse

There are several references, in the hagiographies and mythologies, to Sivam's appearing to various people in various forms. The poet Cekkilar of the twelfth century is the author of *Periyapuranam* (the Great Epic), which narrates the lives of sixty-three *nayanmars.*[70] In his preamble to *Periyapuranam,* Vanmikanathan mentions how twelve of these *nayanmars* attained liberation through worshiping the guru.[71] Most of these appearances are sudden, temporary, and theophanic; they do not seem to have the nuanced understanding of the role and function of the guru as one finds it in the philosophical writings. *Tiruvilaiyatalpuranam* (the Epic of the Sacred Sports), a text written by Parancoti Munivar in the seventeenth century, describes the various heroic and salvific acts of Siva. Since such acts are as fun and play to Siva, they are called the sacred sports of Siva.[72] In these stories Siva does not always appear as a guru. He appears in different forms, fulfills a task, and disappears. So the appearances are occasional and docetic. These stories blur the philosophical distinction between *avatar* and guru.

Several stories do refer to Sivam as taking particular *avatars*. From these considerations we can say that clearly the narrative literature in the Saivite tradition does not understand the saving activity of Sivam, and the role of the guru in it, in the same way as this activity is described in the philosophical writings.

It is quite apparent that Saiva Siddhanta shares certain features of its guru concept with most of the religious traditions in India. The guru is a human being who has reached a higher state in his or her spiritual life. One should always understand the guru in theological terms, that is, in relation to God. Furthermore, such a guru is closely linked with the process of one's achievement of final bliss or salvation.

Yet the Saiva concept of guru has its own peculiar features: First, the concept of guru is seen in opposition to that of *avatar*. The guru is *not* an *avatar*, because Sivam cannot be born. Second, the justice and mercy of God are not set in opposition to each other in the person of the guru. This is different from the Vaishnavite position, which sees Vishnu as the embodiment of justice and the guru as that of mercy.[73] Third, the guru in Tamil Saivism is not tied down to any particular succession of gurus; the choice of a guru, either by a disciple or by the tradition, possesses an open-ended character. Finally, one of the striking features is the repeated emphasis on the divine initiative in the role and function of the guru. It is Sivam who comes as the guru and frees the soul from its impurities. Even the worship of the guru should be undertaken with this in mind. This stands in contrast to the Virasaivite's higher respect for his or her guru than for Sivam.[74]

To sum up, the concept of guru in Saiva Siddhanta operates on three levels of meaning. First, the guru is one who works within the heart of the believer. The guru is not a physical presence, but rather a spiritual one (the level of meaning exemplified in the hymnic discourse). The second level is that of the theophanic and occasional appearance of Sivam as guru. Manikkavacakar's experience of Sivam as guru belongs to this category. This is the level of meaning that is found in the mythological and hagiographical writings. The third level is that which pre-dominates in the philosophical writings. The guru is a human being who has reached a stage of maturation in his or her spiritual journey and functions as Sivam to the believer. This stance repudiates the idea of *avatar* and maintains that the relation between Sivam and the guru is purely functional.

In short, Sivam is guru, and guru is Sivam. For *vinnanakalars* and *piralayakalars*, Sivam is guru. Sivam is the one who enlightens them and liberates them as the inner-being or in a theophanic manifestation. Therefore, Sivam is guru from eternity to eternity. For *sakalars*, however, the guru functions as Sivam; that is, Sivam enlightens the soul, concealing Sivaself in a human guru. Thus the guru is not a mere teacher in the popular meaning of that term; rather, the guru is teacher-initiator-savior.

CHAPTER 3

THE CHRISTOLOGICAL USE OF GURU IN INDIA

As I outlined in chapter 2, the concept of guru in Saiva Siddhanta holds enormous possibilities for devising a contextual christology in Tamilnadu, as well as for enriching and enhancing Western christological understandings. Before we explore those possibilities, however, I need to acknowledge that the title "guru" has already been used for Jesus the Christ in the history of Christianity in India, particularly in Tamilnadu. Both Christians and others have attempted to use the concept of guru to explain the significance of Jesus, setting precedents for the present study. Though I will not go into a thoroughgoing evaluation of these precedents at this stage, I do wish to recognize them as a motivating factor in my own examination of the idea of guru as a christological model.[1]

The point of reference for my analysis in this section is the Saiva Siddhanta concept of guru. As I have already noted, there is no monolithic understanding of guru in Indian religious history and thought. Those who use the concept of guru in christological construction display a range of understandings of the guru's role and function. I will evaluate those christologies on the basis of Saiva Siddhanta, not on the basis of a set of christological criteria. My chief concern here is only to look, from the perspective of Saiva Siddhanta, at the presuppositions concerning guru that govern these christological attempts. I will allude to certain christological questions and problems as such, but will not deal with them in detail.

For convenience and clarity I will classify the material to be considered in this section under five headings: hymnic literature, apologetic discourse, theological discourse, narrative discourse, and pictorial expressions. Let us examine these one by one.

HYMNIC LITERATURE

Any study of the christological use of guru in Tamil Christian hymns needs to begin with a few historical and methodological considerations. At their earliest period of history, the Christian churches in Tamilnadu developed their hymnic expressions solely through the German and English hymns that were translated into Tamil by Christian missionaries. Yet by the nineteenth century Tamil Christian poets had begun to write Christian hymns in Tamil and set them to indigenous music, both classical and folk.[2] These hymns became a significant part of Tamil Christian worship, albeit without replacing the translated hymns from the West. One discovers in these indigenous hymns a repeated use of "guru" as a title for Christ. These poets are very similar to the Saiva bhakti poets in several ways. First, their poetic style and the form their hymns take express the poets' personal devotion to Jesus in the mode of adoration and praise and with the same kind of evangelistic flavor. Second, numerous and varied titles are attributed to God and Jesus in the same way the bhakti poets attribute such titles to Sivam. According to D. Rajarigam, a twentieth-century Tamil Christian theologian,

> The Tamil poets are extravagant in their language in listing the qualities of Jesus Christ, and they compare Him to various things. Krishna Pillai [one of the poets], for instance, describes Jesus Christ, in his *Rakshanya Manoharam,* as the ocean of bliss, the cloud that showers the rain of grace, life-giving medicine, wealth, river from heaven, mountain of salvation, gem of gems, holy teacher, lord of human soul, eternal life and the like.[3]

The material under consideration in this section is enormous. Hundreds of Tamil Christian poets have written hymns in praise of Jesus. Justice cannot possibly be done to all of them. What I plan to do is look at the hymns that are most frequently used by the Christian congregations in Tamilnadu today, especially in the Church of South India and the Lutheran churches. These hymns were first published by the Christian Literature Society of Madras in 1859. This edition has undergone several revisions and enlargements since then.[4]

I have chosen to arrange this section, not according to individual poets and their hymns, but rather on the basis of recurring motifs.

Three central themes recur in this material in relation to the idea of guru, namely Jesus as guru, Holy Spirit as guru, and priests and Christian ministers as gurus. Each of these is examined in turn.

Jesus as Guru

Wherever the Tamil Christian hymns use the term "guru" to refer to Jesus, it is often compounded with other qualifying terms such as "true," "heavenly," "divine," "lord," and *satcitananda* (which means truth, intelligence, and bliss). For example, Vedanayagam Sastriar, one of the more popular poets, writes:

> Lord guru who is all beauty, I praise you![5]

> The great and gracious one, bestow grace
> Sir guru divine![6]

> I worship, I worship,
> I worship the feet of our Lord guru Jesus![7]

Another poet, Marian Upatesiyar, sings:

> O! Thou true guru, Christ, the true guru!
> Life-giving Word, the guru!
> The good guru of eternal joy!
> Heavenly golden guru! Lord![8]

Describing the triumphal entry of Jesus into the city of Jerusalem, the Reverend Devasagayam of Madurai writes:

> The guru who is mighty,
> The guru whose word never fails,
> The guru who is all good,
> The guru of spotless truth,
> The guru full of boon and blessing,
> He is the one, Sir![9]

The christological use of guru in these hymns exhibits a number of important features. Wherever the word "guru" occurs as a title for Jesus, the poets do not explicitly attribute any particular function to

Jesus. In other words, the poets do not go on to explain the implications of the title "guru"; it simply appears as one among the varied titles attributed to Jesus. There is no specific reference to the teaching role of Jesus, and hence the particular significance of "guru" is lost, so to speak, in the multitude of titles.

Second, the term "guru" never occurs as an alternative to *avatar*. The idea of incarnation is taken for granted, and therefore the title "guru" functions rather as a complement or a supplement to *avatar*. This is possible because most of the leading hymn-writers, such as Krishna Pillai and Sastriar, were converts from the Vaishnavite tradition and most of the others came from the popular Hinduism of the villages.

Third, the hymns exhibit a predominance of biblical categories when it comes to expressing the significance of Jesus. The New Testament titles such as "Son of God," "Son of Man," "Messiah," and "Lord" occur repeatedly in these hymns. The word "guru" is never used for Jesus in the Tamil Bible. The word "rabbi," which could possibly be translated "guru," is consistently transliterated rather than translated in the Tamil version of the New Testament. In the translation of John 13:13 ("You call me Teacher and Lord—and you are right, for that is what I am"), the Greek word *didaskalos* is translated as *potakar* (the one who gives the teachings), not as guru. Thus the poets' faithfulness to the New Testament categories does not give room for a fuller exploitation of the concept of guru.

One may ask whether there is a reflective tradition behind the poets' use of "guru" for Jesus. Among the many references to Jesus as guru, only a few occur where rhyme and alliteration (*etukai* and *monai* in Tamil poetry) are used. Therefore one might say that the poets have deliberately chosen the title "guru" for Jesus. However, it is not easy to find out what exactly they had in mind when they made this choice. Since they do not unpack the title at any point, it is difficult to unearth any reflective tradition behind its use.

The Holy Spirit as Guru

One of the most frequently used hymns of adoration to the Trinity ascribes the title "guru" to the Holy Spirit. M. Vedamanickam of Neyyoor writes thus:

> Holy Spirit, I bow to you!
> Heavenly true guru, I bow to you![10]

The previous stanza, which is an adoration of Christ, goes like this:

> Holy *avatara*, I bow to you!
> Savior of the world, I bow to you![11]

Clearly Vedamanickam sees Jesus primarily as the *avatar* of God and then goes on to praise the Holy Spirit as the divine teacher (guru). Though the word "guru" refers to the Holy Spirit in this one hymn alone, there are several other hymns where the Spirit is described as the *jnani* (the wise and knowledge-granting one). Here the understanding of guru is that of a "spiritual" and invisible teacher who enlightens the hearts of believers as indwelling presence.[12]

Interestingly, N. Murugesa Mudaliar, a Saivite scholar, finds the concept of the Holy Spirit in Christian theology to be similar to the idea of guru in Saiva Siddhanta. He writes, "This doctrine of Guru is not a metaphysical speculation but a truth made valid in the experience of saints. It is similar to the doctrine of the Holy Spirit in Christian Theology."[13]

Pastors and Priests as Gurus

Indian Christian hymns also use the word "guru" to denote priests (generally Jewish) and the ministers of the church. Hymns that are written for the ordination service refer to ministers as gurus. For example, Isakku Upatesiyar writes:

> Creating daily in your servant
> Character of purity and truth,
> Graciously establish him
> As guru.[14]

Marian Upatesiyar describes the Bible as the melody that is sung by the preachers and catechists who are gurus.[15]

The hymns that deal with the passion narratives in the Gospels use the word "guru" or *acariyar* to refer to the Jewish priests and high priests alleged to have plotted to kill Jesus. The word *acariyar* is in line with the Tamil Bible, which consistently uses the same word to translate "priest" in the New Testament.

In sum, the Tamil Christian poets do use the title "guru" for Jesus, though not exclusively for him. They refer to the Holy Spirit as guru and the priests and pastors as guru. This diverse use of "guru" means that one cannot easily draw any significant christological conclusions from their usage. However, the poets do not treat the concept of guru as an alternative to *avatar*, even though the form and the mood of the hymns are similar to that of the bhakti poets of the Saiva tradition. This means that the poets are not necessarily using the concept of guru as it is explicated in the reflective tradition within Saivism; rather, they are guided by the popular use of the word "guru."

These hymns are also similar to Christian devotional poems from other parts of India. For example, the well-known Maratha Christian poet, Narayan Vaman Tilak, writes thus in one of his poems:

> Tenderest, Mother-Guru mine
> Saviour, where is love like thine?[16]

In another poem he writes:

> Once I bethought me, Thou my Guru art,
> I thy disciple, humble and apart;
> Sat low before Thee thus, nor ventured near,
> Schooling my mind to reverential fear.[17]

Another example of devotional poetry outside Tamilnadu comes from the hymns of K. Subba Rao, a religious leader in Andhra Pradesh who has started a "Hindu Christian Movement."[18] Subba Rao was brought up in a Hindu home, yet came to revolt against Hindu beliefs and practices. In 1942 he claimed to have had a vision of Christ, which led to a career of preaching and healing. He never joined the established church and has always remained highly critical of institutional Christianity. Most of his writings are in the form of hymns and lyrics. Commenting on Subba Rao's christology, Kaj Baago, a historian of the church in India, has written that

Subba Rao does not follow modern Hinduism in regarding Christ as an *avatar* among other *avataras*. Although he does not explicitly reject the Christian doctrine of the divinity of Christ, he detests the way in which the Church has made Jesus a God of worship. Jesus is not a God, but a loving Guru, the "Gurudev" or "Sadguru" as he calls him. This means more than just a teacher. Jesus is not simply an instructor, but a saviour who seeks the lost and who comes to the sinner.[19]

APOLOGETIC DISCOURSE

From the very beginning, the Christian churches in Tamilnadu have been firmly committed to the task of evangelism. One of the ways in which this evangelism has been carried out is through the publication of tracts and books of a clearly apologetic character.[20] These works deliberately use the concept of guru to explain and defend the decisive significance of Jesus the Christ.

Tracts

Let us look at two Tamil tracts published by the American Madurai Mission, an institution established by the American Board of Commissioners for Foreign Missions at the beginning of the nineteenth century.[21] The American Madurai Mission mainly worked in and around the city of Madurai. Since Madurai is an important Saivite pilgrimage center with a sizable population of Saivites, the mission must have felt the need to address its apologetics to the Saivites. Published with the Saivites in mind, these tracts quote profusely from the writings of Tamil Saivism, scriptural and otherwise. We do not know whether these tracts were written by the American missionaries themselves or in collaboration with local Christians, since the tracts are anonymous.

The author of the tract entitled *The Dawn of Wisdom* begins by quoting several poems by Agastiyar, one of the siddhars.[22] The siddhars belong to a group of poets and theologians who criticized the Saivite theistic tradition from within.[23] Their poems reflect an invitation to move away from the repressive brahmanical influences in Hinduism to the true gurus who could lead the people to a religion

freed from superstition and empty ritualism. The author quotes one
of Agastiyar's poems thus:

> The One, the Light of the world,
> Who formed this earth in a moment,
> And created humans with qualities
> Thereafter appeared in this world
> Coming as guru
> And showed austerities as an ascetic,
> Without a family or a people to own,
> And departed to the wide heavens
> Appointing the loving siddhars—
> Him you shall worship and take refuge in![24]

This poem mentions the need for turning to the true guru. The author
of the tract takes this as the starting point and goes on to list the
marks of a true guru as divinity, humanity, truth, miraculous power,
generosity, meekness, patience, love, mercy, devotion to God, faithfulness to the Scriptures, omniscience, and compassion toward all
living beings.[25] The next stage in the tract is to elaborate on how
Jesus Christ fulfills all the requirements of a true guru and how Siva
does not. The Saivite understanding of Siva as guru is criticized and
rejected on the basis of the questionable moral character of Siva as
portrayed in the mythologies. The tract ends with an invitation to
turn away from false gurus and turn to the true guru—Jesus Christ—
in order to reach heaven.

Another tract, *Hinduism's Own Witness,* is part of a collection of
tracts entitled *Select Tracts,* published by the American Madurai
Mission.[26] It follows a pattern of argument similar to that of *Dawn
of Wisdom.* However, there are two distinctive features. First, this
tract is more extensive in its criticism of Hinduism, vigorously
condemning both Hindu theological ideas and social customs. It
attacks, for example, idolatry, the caste system, astrology, and the
superiority of Brahmans. Second, the tract makes an interesting
distinction between two types of gurus. The two types are *kariya
guru* and *karana guru.* The *kariya guru* is a guru who does everything
for his own gain and glorifies rituals and ceremonies. The *karana
guru,* on the other hand, is one who does only that which will help
the disciple reach heaven. He sees himself only as a means to the end,

which is union with God (*karana* means instrumental). With this distinction, the author attempts to establish that Jesus is the only *karana guru* who is utterly selfless, even to the extent of giving his life on the cross.[27]

Books and Booklets

The first example of this literature at which we will look is a book entitled *The Bazaar Book,* written by Henry Martyn Scudder, an American missionary in Tamilnadu in the nineteenth century.[28] He wrote it as a companion book for vernacular preachers who found themselves in situations of defending the Christian faith over against the beliefs and practices of Hinduism in general and Tamil Saivism in particular. Thus the book's character is thoroughly apologetic. As Scudder himself acknowledges:

> Most of these addresses assume, as a starting point, some prominent falsity in Hinduism, which is exhibited and refuted as an introduction to the opposite truth; and such truth is, in each instance, displayed in connection with Him who said, "I am the way, the truth and the life."[29]

The author begins by establishing the universal human need for a guru, bringing in various quotations from the Saivite writings to establish this point. Four reasons are given to justify this need, namely, the impermanence of human life, the lack of knowledge, the lack of any merit on the part of humans, and the total absence of true joy.[30] This explication of the reasons for the need of a guru leads Scudder to assert that "it is within the province of God alone to sustain and enlighten us, to rescue us from sin and fill us with joy. Hence it is plain, that God himself must come to be our Guru."[31]

From here Scudder moves on to show that neither Siva nor Vishnu can fulfill this human need, since the mythologies concerning Siva and Vishnu portray them as beings with a low moral character, and since most of these stories border on obscenity. From such a vantage point, the author finds it easy to move to a position of presenting Jesus as the true "God-Guru incarnate." The address ends in a judgmental note: "Oh! People! It is because you know not this true Guru [Jesus Christ], that you worship stocks and stones."[32]

The book *Siva Bhakti: with an Examination of the Siddhanta Philosophy*, by American missionary John Murdoch, is addressed to educated Hindus, namely those Saivites who have had Western education.[33] Murdoch carries out a detailed and historical study of Saiva Siddhanta and attempts to expose the fallacies in Saivism, and thus to prepare the educated Saivites to accept Jesus Christ as the true guru. His criticism of Saiva Siddhanta is based on two criteria: compatibility with modern science and faithfulness to Christianity as the religion of revelation. For example, he ends his discussion of the errors in Saiva Siddhanta thus: "For the above and other reasons the Siddhanta cannot be accepted as the revelation from God, but as the invention of men in an unenlightened age."[34] By dismissing Saiva Siddhanta as fallacious and contrary to the revelation from God, which is only available in Jesus Christ, Murdoch is able to state that "the name of the *Sadguru,* the true divine teacher, is JESUS CHRIST."[35] He does not explicate this statement further, but rather launches into an examination of the two main teachings of Jesus, "the Fatherhood of God" and "the Brotherhood of man," as the distinctive features of Christianity. Murdoch sees these two teachings as peculiar to Christianity, and that which distinguishes it from Saiva Siddhanta.

One needs to note with appreciation the effort of the early missionaries to speak to the religious situation in Tamilnadu. They were right in recognizing the importance of Saivite religious thought as a vehicle for expressing the significance of Jesus. However, one should not fail to notice the problems inherent in the kind of apologetic approach that the missionaries took. The portrayal of Saiva Siddhanta in these materials is almost a deliberate caricature of Saivism. The best element in the Saivite tradition—its reflective and well-conceived philosophical tradition—is not taken seriously by the missionaries. Moreover, by exploiting the writings of the siddhars, the authors of these tracts and books fail to recognize that the criticism that is offered is from within the Saivite tradition, and not one that calls for an alternative religious tradition. In this sense the missionaries lack an in-depth study of the Tamil Saivite history and tradition. Such a superficial understanding of Hinduism was present in almost all the Western missionary activity in India during the nineteenth century. According to Pathak, an Indian historian,

A careful reader is struck by the sense of missionary writers on the bright sides of Hindu thought and culture. The sublime philosophy of the Gita and the Upanishads was hardly discussed. The ideals enshrined in the characters of Ramayan which have captured Indian imagination from times immemorial, were never mentioned. . . . It was a favorite strategy of missionary writers to compare Krishna with Christ and show the superiority of the latter's character.[36]

One also discovers that while criticizing certain Saivite beliefs on the basis of modern science, the missionaries refrained from using the same criterion for Christian doctrines. At that point they switched to another set of criteria, based on the presupposition that only in Christianity does one encounter God's revelation. To add to the problem, there is an underlying imperialistic conviction in these writings that the civilization of the West is superior to that of India. I am not making a value judgment on the missionaries themselves, but note only the fact that they were victims of the imperialistic political values of their day. For example, Murdoch opens his examination of Saiva Siddhanta by saying that the civilized nations reject the fables formerly believed, and that they have higher ideas of morality.[37] By "civilized nations," Murdoch means the nations of the West.

THEOLOGICAL DISCOURSE

Indian Christian writings examined in this section are more reflective and systematic than the hymnic or apologetic literature. One discovers in these writings a definite christological exploration, undertaken with the aid of the concept of guru.[38]

Hindu Thinkers

RAJA RAMMOHAN ROY   Rammohan Roy was a Hindu reformer, thinker, and writer in the nineteenth century who pioneered a liberal reform within Hinduism. He was motivated by a spirit of Indian nationalism.[39] He had been greatly influenced in his youth by both

Islam and Christianity. As M. M. Thomas, an Indian Christian theologian, writes:

> Rammohan Roy had three fundamental ideas in his religion: first, a monotheistic faith in the unity of God inspired fundamentally perhaps by Islam; secondly, the conviction that morality is the essence of true religion; . . . and thirdly, a certain rationalism which, while conscious of its limits, still demands that religion should hold only beliefs which are reasonable, and that reason should serve to purify religion of superstition and unnecessary mysteries and miracles.[40]

With these presuppositions about religion, Rammohan Roy was attracted to the teachings of Jesus and saw them as "a guide to peace and happiness." Therefore, in 1820 he published a book entitled *The Precepts of Jesus, the Guide to Peace and Happiness, Extracted from the Books of the New Testament, Ascribed to the Four Evangelists.*[41] This publication triggered a heated theological dialogue between Roy and Joshua Marshman, a Christian missionary at Serampore in West Bengal. Roy published three "Appeals" to the Christian public in answer to Marshman's charges. Roy approached the problem of christology from a liberal humanistic point of view, whereas Marshman did so from a strictly Christian doctrinal perspective. As S. J. Samartha, a Christian theologian in India, writes, "Ram Mohan Roy was motivated more by the desire to build a new secular humanity in India than faithfulness to the established doctrines of Christianity." "His [Roy's] frank emphasis on the teachings of Jesus Christ as the guide to peace and happiness should be regarded as arising from the quest for resources to build up a new humanity in India."[42]

Rammohan Roy portrayed Jesus as a divine teacher. In several of his writings he named Jesus the divine teacher, the best among all others. He deliberately attempted to separate the teachings of Jesus from the doctrines concerning the divine nature of Christ as explicated in the ecclesiastical creeds. He saw this separation as essential to making the teachings of Jesus more forceful and appealing to the Indian mind.

> I feel persuaded that by separating from the other matters contained in the New Testament, the moral precepts found in this book, these

will be more likely to produce the desirable effect of improving the hearts and minds of men of different persuasions and degrees of understanding.[43]

With his attention on reforming Hinduism of its polytheism and idolatry, "he did not wish to place Jesus Christ alongside the pantheon of Puranic gods."[44]

Rammohan Roy did use the titles "savior," "redeemer," and "mediator" for Christ, but with the qualification that these do not in any way refer to the deity of Christ.[45] His was a purely functional approach to the question of christology, which saw the primary task of christology as providing a "guide to peace and happiness." When he was pressed by Marshman to face the question of the "person" of Christ, Roy opted for the natural inferiority of the Son to the Father, bringing in ample evidences from the New Testament to support his position. As Samartha writes, "Therefore, according to Ram Mohan Roy, the oneness of God and Christ is the oneness of harmony of will and purpose, not of identity in nature or being."[46]

Rammohan Roy's idea of divine teacher, though it resembles the concept of guru, lacks the aspect of personal devotion to the guru that is an integral part of the Saiva Siddhanta concept of guru. In his view the precepts take precedence over the preceptor. As a liberal humanist Roy was suspicious of the bhakti tradition within Hinduism, which is one of the reasons why he limits the precepts of Jesus to the Synoptic Gospels alone.[47] One may conjecture that he was using the idea of teacher in its secular and Western usage, rather than "guru" with its Hindu religious underpinnings.

MAHATMA GANDHI Gandhi was attracted to Jesus mainly through the Sermon on the Mount and the idea of nonviolence he found there. It was the teaching of Jesus that caught Gandhi's attention; any attachment to the person of Jesus was on the basis of his embodying and acting out what he taught, especially the principle of nonviolence. Moreover, Gandhi's ideas were shaped by the needs of the day, namely, India's struggle for political independence. In his attempt to provide spiritual foundations for a secular political involvement such as the struggle for independence, the teachings of Jesus became a great source of inspiration to Gandhi. As a genuine Hindu, Gandhi believed that all the religions of the world were essentially and equally true. Therefore the doctrine of the deity and finality of Christ was a position unacceptable to Gandhi.

Gandhi's writings were sporadic and occasional, motivated by specific needs and particular situations. To examine his view of Jesus, I shall mainly depend on the book *What Jesus Means to Me,* a collection of Gandhi's sayings on Christ and Christianity.[48] Gandhi never failed to recognize Jesus as one of the great teachers of the world. He wrote:

> I could accept Jesus as a martyr, an embodiment of sacrifice, and a divine teacher, but not as the most perfect man ever born.[49]

> I regard Jesus as a great teacher of humanity, but I do not regard him as the only begotten son of God.[50]

> What, then, does Jesus mean to me? To me, He was one of the greatest teachers humanity has ever had.[51]

Gandhi, like Rammohan Roy, separated the teachings of Jesus from the doctrines concerning him, laying emphasis on the former alone. Though he acknowledged the historicity of Jesus, Gandhi did not see the historical Jesus as vital to the efficacy of his teachings. He wrote:

> I may say that I have never been interested in a historical Jesus. I should not care if it was proved by some one that the man called Jesus never lived, and that what was narrated in the Gospels was a figment of the writer's imagination. For the Sermon on the Mount would still be true for me.[52]

Though Gandhi refers to Jesus as the divine teacher, the dominant model is that of an embodiment or an example of the principle of nonviolence. Jesus is the "supreme *satyagrahi* [one who lives by and for Truth]." As a supreme example, the person of Christ is able to renew human life. Gandhi wrote:

> An example of this flowering [of compassion and goodness] may be found in the figure and in the life of Jesus. . . . The lives of all have, in

some greater or lesser degree, been changed by His presence, His actions, and the words spoken by His divine voice.[53]

It is clear that Gandhi does not operate with the Hindu religious view of guru; rather, his view is similar to that of Rammohan Roy, who views Jesus as a great teacher who embodied what he taught.

SRI PARANANDA   Ponnambalam Ramanathan, otherwise known as Sri Parananda, was a solicitor general of Ceylon. He was a Saivite thinker who wrote commentaries on the Gospels of Matthew and John from a Saiva Siddhanta perspective.[54] Parananda's portrayal of Jesus is that of a "true teacher of the kingdom of God."[55] For him, "Jesus was above all things a teacher."[56]

Because his writings were in English, Parananda never used the word "guru" as such. But we can be sure that he is operating with the concept of guru in Saiva Siddhanta because his commentaries were written with a specifically Saiva Siddhanta perspective. In his commentary on the Gospel of John, Parananda identifies the Logos with the idea of guru.

> This All-pervading Power of Direction [Logos] is the great *Informer of the Universe,* the Power that *forms* and *shapes* every entity, mental and material, and everything in that entity according to its needs. . . . Hence It is the Teacher of the Universe. As in all things, so in man, It stands *within* and *without* him.[57]

True to Saiva Siddhanta, Parananda rejects the idea of incarnation and interprets John 1:14 ("The Word became flesh") in the following manner:

> Having already explained that the translation of ver. 14 should not be "the Word was made flesh" but "the Word appeared in flesh," it is needless to point out that "manifestation" alone (i Tim. iii, 16) and no "incarnation," is meant by it; for *Incarnation* or *Enfleshment* of the Holy Spirit occurred long before Its "manifestation" was vouch-safed to man. . . . The Holy Spirit of God within the form of Sanctified Man appeared as Teacher of Truth to men who had become ripe for sanctification or Peace.[58]

Here is a genuine attempt to work out a christology on the basis of the concept of guru in Saiva Siddhanta. For Parananda, the Holy Spirit is the teacher within the soul of the human, and Jesus is a teacher without. Yet since Parananda's christological exploration is tied to an exposition of the Gospels, it raises more problems of exegesis and hermeneutics, instead of offering us a constructive proposal. Commenting on Parananda's work, A. J. Appasamy, an Indian Christian theologian, writes:

> An exclusively Indian meaning need not be read into a book that was written in another land in a different environment, as is done in Sri Parananda's *Commentary on the Gospel,* where the writer makes John out to be a Hindu following the Saiva Siddhanta doctrine. To do this is to go against the fundamental laws of historical criticism.[59]

Parananda's project also raises the more serious question whether or not one should see the christological task as mere hermeneutics of New Testament christologies. I will discuss this particular issue later when I define the task of christology.

Christian Theologians

ROBERTO DE NOBILI   As a young Jesuit missionary, Roberto de Nobili came to India in 1605 to work in and around Madurai.[60] He adapted his life-style, as much as possible, to that of an Indian ascetic and pioneered the use of Tamil terms for the explication of Christian theological concepts. According to S. Rajamanickam, the compiler of de Nobili's writings,

> Nobili coined the terms for Christian theology and prepared a proper vehicle for conveying Christian ideas. He christianized certain words and infused into them a new meaning. . . . The Christian message became incarnate in Tamil thanks to his efforts.[61]

The concept of guru is one of the models de Nobili found useful in explicating the significance of Jesus. According to a Tamil Jesuit theologian, "De Nobili's specific contribution to Christology seems to be his concept of Christ as divine guru."[62]

De Nobili begins his christology with the doctrine of the incarnation as it has been traditionally interpreted in the creeds of the church. He devotes several sections in his writings to a discussion of this theological idea.[63] His book on the life of Christ has the title, *The Life of the Lord Jesus Who Is Both True God and True Man.*[64] De Nobili's use of guru is over and above that of the Western concept of incarnation. But for him the idea of *avatar* was not the same as incarnation in the Christian tradition. He argued, on the basis of the differences between *avatar* and incarnation, that Christ is the true incarnation of God.[65]

De Nobili used the phrases *tivviya guru* (divine guru), *sarguru* (true guru), *tevaguru* (God-guru), and so on. His use of these concepts held two emphases. First, when he applies the title "guru" to Jesus, he clearly has the teaching role of Jesus in mind. The idea of ignorance is a primary component in de Nobili's concept of sin, a fact readily seen in the numerous metaphors he uses. For example, he describes human sinfulness as a man who chooses a ball of clay instead of a diamond, and as one who clings to the mirage rather than water to quench his thirst.[66] He also describes human sin as "forgetting" the way of God.[67] Thus the divine guru Jesus is one who teaches the way to "moksha," or final liberation. Second, de Nobili describes Jesus as a guru who initiates the disciple into the recitation of the divine *mantiram* (*mantra,* the sacred formula). In his discussion of the Lord's Prayer, de Nobili prescribes it as the *mantra* for the Christian disciple.[68] So Jesus is both a teacher and an initiator, that is, a guru.

Apart from his christological use of guru, de Nobili uses the word "guru" also to refer to the ministers of the Christian church and the apostles. The apostle Peter is the chief guru.[69] The idea of "apostolic succession" is explained through the concept of *guruparamparai* or *guru marapu.*[70]

It is interesting to see that de Nobili uses the concept of *incarnation* when he discusses the nature of the person of Christ, and opts for "guru" in his discussion of the function or work of Christ in the scheme of salvation. So de Nobili's christology is a combination of *incarnation* and guru. At the time of incarnation, God spoke to the soul of Christ, according to de Nobili, in this manner: "With body I am sending you to the world. There going about as a guru, show all men clearly by your conduct and words, that they must renounce all that is sin and that they must walk in the path of virtue so that they may attain the shores."[71]

V. CHAKKARAI   V. Chakkarai was a lay theologian in South India who had converted to Christianity from the Vaishnavite bhakti tradition. He was actively involved in the political life of India as a lawyer, as mayor of Madras (1941), and as chairman of the All India Trade Union Congress (1951). He is well known for his two books, *Jesus the Avatar* and *The Cross and Indian Thought,* which treat christology and soteriology, respectively.[72] He was also the author of several articles in contemporary Christian journals.

Chakkarai works out his christology primarily in the context of the Hindu concept of *avatar,* especially from the Tamil Vaishnavite bhakti tradition. In discussing his choice of *avatar* as a workable christological model, Chakkarai takes up the concept of guru in Saiva Siddhanta only to reject it as being unsuitable for christological exploration. His reason for doing so is that the Saiva Siddhanta concept refers to a mere appearance of humanity in the sense of a theophany. "Siva is said to assume a human form for a time and achieves some object. These are merely appearances of humanity, without the reality."[73] Summing up his examination of the concept of guru in Saiva Siddhanta, Chakkarai writes: "In all these instances of divine revelation God stands, as it were, outside man's consciousness and inspires him with some divine message or renders him some needed help."[74]

Chakkarai's preference for the concept of *avatar* is based on his emphasis on the need for a more intimate union between God and humanity, which for him is a soteriological necessity. For Chakkarai the idea of guru does not bring to light this close interconnection between the divine and the human. Thus he indicates that one needs to go beyond the idea of Jesus as guru to do full justice to the personality of Jesus.[75] In another place he uses the title "guru" for the Holy Spirit: "The Spirit is represented in the Fourth Gospel as the Paraclete, the Consoler, the great Guru and Revealer."[76]

I would point out here that Chakkarai's understanding of the Saiva Siddhanta concept of guru is largely informed by the narrative tradition within Tamil Saivism; he does not explore the Saivite philosophical writings. Such an exploration might have given him a positive appreciation of the christological possibilities in the concept of guru.

A. J. APP ASAMY Bishop A. J. Appasamy of the Church of South India was one of the leading Tamil Christian theologians of this century. One of his early writings, *The Gospel and India's Heritage*, contains a discussion of the possibility of using "guru" as a title for Jesus.[77] The chapter "The Teachings of Jesus on God" opens:

> We may begin our study of Him [Jesus] by regarding Him as a great religious teacher *(Guru)*. His demands from us are the same as the requirements of any *Guru*, a readiness to learn from Him and to spread His teaching. This is the idea with which we may well start.[78]

Thus Appasamy finds the guru concept to be a workable starting point for an Indian christology. He lists nine qualifications required of a guru as found in *Nannul,* an early Tamil grammar book. These qualifications include good ancestry, love of humanity, knowledge of God, possession of dignity, clearness of thought, gift of speech, power of consistency, understanding of the world's ways, and lofty character.[79] He goes on to establish how Jesus fulfills all the requirements prescribed by *Nannul.* As he moves to discuss the various other aspects of the life and ministry of Jesus, Appasamy finds that, though the concept of guru is a good christological starting point, it is not adequate for a full-blown christology. In chapter 13, where he describes Jesus as the incarnation of God, he states that

> we started out on this inquiry with the question "Who is Jesus?" We have sought to answer it in various ways. He was a devoted *Bhakta.* . . . He was an ideal *Guru* possessing all the qualifications which are expected of a religious teacher. . . . In describing Him as a *Bhakta,* as a *Guru,* and as a Suffering Servant we feel we have not adequately described Him. He was more than any of these.[80]

Moreover, Appasamy maintains that Jesus' teaching was of a consistently higher order than that of other gurus, and that no other guru had lived in complete harmony with his own teaching as Jesus did.[81] In addition, both the claims of Jesus concerning his unique relationship to God and the claims of the church about Jesus' person on the basis of its experience of Jesus call for a vision of Christ that is more than that of guru. Thus Appasamy moves to consider the Hindu concept of *avatar,* comparing it with the Christian idea of incarnation, and accepting it as a christological model with certain qualifications.

Toward the end of this book, Appasamy discusses the Saiva Siddhanta's criticism of *avatar* and criticizes Saiva Siddhanta on two counts. First he maintains that the Saivite vision of guru is docetic. Second, if one believes that God is Love, then one should be prepared to see God's love in action to the extent of God's becoming a human being in order to save humanity.

> It is surprising that the *Saiva Siddhanta* takes up such a position [of docetism]. It believes fully in a God of Love. It also believes that this God of Love, out of His boundless compassion comes to the world to help His devotees. But it does not go further. The Christian belief is that love goes further. God identified Himself entirely with men. He was born as a child.[82]

BRAHMABANDHAB UPADHYAYA   Upadhyaya was another Indian Christian theologian who used the guru concept as a starting point for an Indian christology.[83] In an article titled "Christ's Claims to Attention," Upadhyaya writes that "the first, though not the foremost, claim of Christ is His position as the Teacher Universal. He commissioned His apostles to teach *all* nations to observe *all* things whatsoever He had commanded them, and promised to be with them *all* days."[84] Though Upadhyaya does not use the term "guru" as such, one can detect that the concept of guru is implied in his idea of "Teacher Universal." In the passage just quoted, his emphasis falls more on the universal character of Jesus' teachings than on the teaching role of Jesus. Thus Christ has a claim to attention due to the universal appeal of his teachings.

Upadhyaya mentions two more claims of Christ: "his unfolding of the mystery of God's inner life" and his divinity.[85] Having explained these two claims, Upadhyaya ends his article thus:

> I have stated the chief claims of Jesus Christ. His position as Teacher Universal, His revelation of the very *sanctum sanctorum* of the Divine Life, His saving atonement by becoming one with humanity in sorrow

and weakness that may be united to Divinity, deserve, I trust, respectful and patient attention.[86]

Commenting on Upadhyaya's employment of the concept of guru, J. B. Chettimattam, a Roman Catholic theologian in India, writes:

> One who made the Concept of Guru applied to Christ the corner stone of his Indian Christian theology was Brahmabandhav Upadhyaya. . . . [For him] Christ is the unique Guru who being himself God and totally sinless, comes to the level of man. . . . This is the essence of Christian experience for Brahmabandhav.[87]

I would raise a question about Chettimattam's judgment in this regard. Upadhyaya's christology operates mainly with the idea of Christ as the incarnate Logos, even though he uses the concept of guru as a starting point. He attempted to bring a creative synthesis between the Thomistic system of thought and the Advaita philosophy of Sankara. In another essay, Upadhyaya writes:

> Jesus Christ is God by the necessity of His being, but He became man of His own free choice. His birth did not depend upon man's will. It was compassion for us which made Him our Brother, like us in sorrow and suffering, but without sin. Jesus Christ is perfectly Divine and perfectly human. He is the incarnate Logos.[88]

Thus Upadhyaya's use of the guru concept is marginal, and different from the Saiva Siddhanta concept of guru, which functions as an alternative to the idea of incarnation.

J. B. CHETTIMATTAM J. B. Chettimattam is a Roman Catholic theologian in India. His theological thinking has taken shape in the context of relating the Christian faith to the Advaita philosophy of Hinduism, and in an attempt to promote a dialogue between Christian and Advaita personal consciousness and mystical experience. He envisions "theology as human interiority."[89] Chettimattam notes how several Indian thinkers have used the concept of guru to highlight the ethico-religious dimensions of Christian existence. While appreciating such attempts, he suggests that one should envision Christ the guru more as a "presence" than as an example.

The most significant aspect of the Guru as applies to Christ is the effective divine presence it implies. Guru is a presence, an intensely energizing personal presence, or rather a supra-personal presence. For the Sishya the Guru is identical in function with God, because he opens up a personal relationship that embraces all persons in a single mystery of the supra-personal Absolute.[90]

Thus Chettimattam finds Christ as the one guru who is "God's decisive, eschatological, and soteriological presence to the individual."[91] Here again I find that "guru" functions not as an alternative to *avatar* but rather as a complement to it. Furthermore, Chettimattam emphasizes the "spiritual" and "interior" character of Christ's presence when he uses "guru" as a title for Christ. This is clearly seen in the passage with which he ends his discussion:

The task of theology is not to create a well constructed system of concepts and principles but rather to point out the intimate relevance of the mysteries to the personal life and fulfillment of men. Here the personality of the Guru, the prophet, the teacher, leader, and saviour constitutes the forms of ethico-religious plan of life presented to all men. But the work of liberation or salvation should take place in the individual person. . . . The positive process is one of deepening one's own personal consciousness, which finally discovers its fullness in the transcendent light of God, in the interpersonal Communion of the Trinity.[92]

XAVIER IRUDHAYARAJ   Xavier Irudhayaraj, another Roman Catholic theologian, is the only Indian theologian who has attempted to use the Saivite concept of guru, consciously and deliberately, for christological purposes. However, he has not worked out such a christology in detail. In an article titled "Christ—the Guru," he outlines the possibility of using guru as a christological model.[93]

In the same article, Irudhayaraj surveys the guru concept in the Hindu tradition and finds that guru and God are closely related. Out of his survey three main points emerge:

First, the absolute need of the guru in the process of attaining liberation; secondly, the divine character of the guru, so that "only that knowledge which issues from the lips of the guru is alive"; thirdly, the fact that Siva himself is the Guru who instructs through all the earthly gurus.[94]

He goes on to construct what he calls a "theology of the guru."

> The divine character of the guru can be studied and its implications, including its incarnation dimensions, examined. This would be a speculative and dogmatic approach. Or one could compare and contrast the guru title with such biblical titles of Christ as Rabbi, Rabboni, Master, Prophet, etc. This would imply a thorough analysis of both the traditions, which cannot be attempted here. We intend to pursue a simpler way, and offer certain observations born of Christian reflection on the Hindu theology of the guru.[95]

Thus, without going into the details of a fully developed guru-christology, Irudhayaraj presents us with certain possibilities within such a christology, and invites us to explore further. These possibilities are fourfold: First, the relational character of the guru-sisya model can bring out the idea of Christ as "the sacrament of every *Guru-Sisya* dialogue." Second, Jesus, seen as guru, is both mediator and revealer of our divine sonship. Third, this kind of christology, though rooted in the personal and the individual, has potential for the "inter-personal as well." "Since according to Saiva Siddhanta all gurus are manifestations of Siva, there is among all the *sisyas* a basic community of experience."[96] Fourth, the idea of Christian fellowship can be seen as "the fruit of discipleship." In another article Irudhayaraj describes the guru-sisya model as having great potential for an Indian ecclesiology.[97]

Irudhayaraj, unlike the other Christian theologians, does not use the concept of guru as a mere starting point, but envisions it rather as a third and complementary approach to the metaphysical and functional approaches to christology. He writes:

> Unlike the *metaphysical* (two natures and one person: Chalcedon) and *functional* (Scholastic soteriology) approaches to Christology, the Guru-Sisya-tradition inspires us to focus on the mystical approach to the person of Christ, based on the experience of His personal love and grace (since Guru is the transparently divine communicator of grace). Such a *complementary* approach in Christology would help us to see

that the Guru-Sisya bond symbolizes the intimate and immediate relation between Christ and the faithful. . . . Indeed Christ is the *Sad-Guru* and the baptized are His chosen disciples who must always sit and listen at the feet of the Master and Lord.[98]

NARRATIVE DISCOURSE

In this section we deal with an entirely different kind of literature. These are writings that come to us in the form of autobiographical accounts of Christians from the West who were gripped by the concept of guru. Because of their narrative character these writings do not fully elaborate the christological possibilities of the guru concept. Yet references to such possibilities manifest themselves here and there in these writings. Two books that illustrate this body of narrative discourse are *Guru Jesus* and *Guru and Disciple*.

Guru Jesus

Robert Van de Weyer was an Englishman who toured India several times and met with different Hindu gurus in India. Though he began his journeys as a liberal, atheistic humanist, he came to a fresh commitment to Jesus through the model of Jesus as guru. His book *Guru Jesus,* an account of his spiritual journey, contains the following statement in its introduction:

> As the title indicates, I became a follower of Jesus, by regarding him as a Guru. I recognized him as a supremely wise and happy man, and, in the Hindu tradition, gave him my complete and unquestioning obedience so that he could show me the way to wisdom and happiness.[99]

In describing how he was gripped by the idea of guru, Van de Weyer discusses the reasons for having a *single* guru.[100] First, only under a single teacher can one "reasonably take the high risks and hardships which the spiritual life demands." Second, "It is better to concentrate all your efforts in learning to love and trust a single teacher than diffusing them on several." Third, only a single teacher's instructions are consistent, because they are all based on that one person's experience. Fourth, "It is far better to become immersed in the language and symbols of one particular teacher rather than grapple vainly with lots of different languages."

Having been convinced of the need for a single teacher, Van de Weyer decided to experiment with making Jesus his guru for a test period of six months. He writes: "During this time I shall act as full disciple, studying his teachings closely and following them as far as I can, regardless of whether I fully understand or agree with them."[101] The experiment helped Van de Weyer to find a way to peace and happiness through Jesus the guru.

Certain features of this account call for our attention. First, Van de Weyer's idea of guru does not see the relationship between God and the guru the way it is seen in Saiva Siddhanta, because he bypasses the question of the divinity of the guru:

> To make Jesus your Guru is . . . to believe primarily in the human being who teaches and whose own attainment of interior joy validates his teachings.[102]

At another stage in the story Van de Weyer writes:

> Such phrases as "the Son of God" and "God Incarnate" which are virtually meaningless to me have, I suppose, cluttered my conception of him, and made it impossible for me to conceive of having direct relationship with him. Yet why can't I think of Jesus Christ just as a man, as a very wise and happy man, who may be able to show me the path to happiness?[103]

Second, the dominant motif in Van de Weyer's guru concept is the idea of absolute obedience required of a disciple by the guru. This is an obedience that is unquestioning and undivided, with or without understanding. It is the kind of obedience that is advocated in most of the popular guru movements, but it is not explicitly recommended by Saiva Siddhanta. The Saivite idea of personal and worshipful devotion to the guru can be less oppressive than the absolute obedience recommended here.

Guru and Disciple

Henri Le Saux, popularly known as Swami Abhishiktananda (1910–1973), wrote an account of his life in his book *Guru and Disciple*.[104] The account, "A Sage from the East," is a narrative that "aims at being a straightforward account of the teaching and way of life of a Hindu sage, without any attempt at comparison or evaluation from a Christian point of view."[105] Abhishiktananda was a Roman Catholic theologian who worked mainly with the traditional Logos-christology, expressing it through the monistic and mystical language of Vedanta. He advocated a dialogue between Hindus and Christians in the meeting of hearts, in the very depth of a mystical experience of unity with God. Moreover, Abhishiktananda saw in Christ the fulfillment and culmination of Hindu mysticism.[106]

In *Guru and Disciple*, Abhishiktananda explicates the concept of guru as it was taught to him by Swami Gnanananda.[107] Only once does a reference to Jesus as guru appear.

> Suddenly Vanya stopped in the midst of his story and, his heart filled with sadness, continued, "Do you now see why the word of western preachers so seldom penetrates the Hindu soul? Yet the Christ whom they proclaim is the guru *par excellence*. His voice resounds throughout the world for those who have ears to hear and, more important still, he reveals himself in the secret cave of the heart of man!"[108]

Yet the concept of guru is not a dominant christological model in the full corpus of Abhishiktananda's theological writings, nor are its christological possibilities drawn out any further here.

PICTORIAL EXPRESSIONS

By pictorial expressions, I mean paintings of Jesus by Indian artists, Christians and others. Since the time of the Moghul empire (sixteenth century C.E.), there have been Indian paintings of Jesus.[109] What I attempt to do is to look at those paintings which seem to explicate the significance of Jesus in ways that are similar to the concept of guru. It should be noted first, however, that the paintings under consideration here do not represent the common people's view of Christ. The common people's view of Christ is largely informed by Western paintings and the so-called bazaar pictures (commercial and popular), most fashionable among these being the paintings of the sacred heart and the crucifixion. Some of the popular paintings depict Christ, Buddha, and Gandhi together. As R. W. Taylor, a historian of Indian Christian art, writes: "They [the popular pictures] must be taken seriously even when the Babe is a blue-eyed blonde, as He often is, and even when they are treated as almost magical—as they very often are."[110] But none of these popular pictures deals with the idea of Jesus as guru, except the ones that portray Jesus along with Buddha and Gandhi.

Second, even the most creative and innovative Indian artists deal only with a limited number of themes in the life of Jesus, such as the Nativity and the Crucifixion. Third, since I do not have access to what the painters themselves were trying to communicate through their paintings, I must rely on what art historians tell us about the possible interpretations of these paintings. This being the case, it is difficult to come to any definite conclusions regarding the christologies that inform the various paintings.

There is only one Indian painting titled *Guru*. This painting is by Sister Genevieve, a Roman Catholic nun in India. Commenting on her painting, Taylor writes:

> In her "Guru," . . . Christ wears the same garments [as in other paintings] and the long garment is white, the clinch red and the shawl saffron—all of which makes Him look almost too much like a theologically fashionable young bishop (although I suppose that Sister Genevieve probably would not give even such a bishop the gold aura surrounding body and the halo that He has here).[111]

Thus, Sister Genevieve's concept of guru is more informed by the popular use of guru for Christian priests than by the Hindu theological tradition.

A study of the portraits of Jesus in the paintings of other Indian artists reveals that the idea of guru or teacher is one of the controlling images in them.[112] According to Arno Lehmann, another historian of Indian Christian art, "The holy figures and holy story are placed in Indian settings, and Indian symbolism is being employed. Christ himself appears as a Guru. . . . The lotus stands out as the symbol of peace and purity."[113] The guruship of Jesus is portrayed in two ways. First, the figure of Jesus is that of a *rishi*, a *sadhu*, or a *yogi*.[114] For example, Alfred Thomas's paintings of the life of Christ exhibit this kind of depiction of guruship.[115] The painting of the hand gestures of Jesus in the language of the different *mudras* (gestures in Indian classical dance) also attempts to portray the ideas of the guruship of Jesus. *Abhaya mudra* (refuge-giving gesture) and *varada mudra* (boon-conferring gesture) are often used. In the frontispiece of the Chapel at Dharmaram College at Bangalore, *jnana mudra* (wisdom-granting gesture) is deliberately used to portray Jesus as the guru.[116] On the basis of these *mudras* one can say that the role of Jesus as guru is seen as bringing together the *jnana* and the bhakti traditions in the concept of guru.

This discussion of pictorial or artistic expressions leads us merely to the observation that the christological use of guru finds its place in Indian paintings of Jesus as well. A more detailed examination of the meaning of these paintings requires a level of study beyond the scope of the present work.

To conclude this survey of the christological use of guru in India, let me make the following observations.

1) The concept of guru has been one of the significant models for understanding the person and work of Christ in India, right from Christianity's inception there. It has been operative in all five modes of discourse I have discussed.

2) In unreflective and nonconceptual discourses, I find that those who use the title "guru" for Jesus do so with comfort and ease. This is so because the title "guru" occurs among a multitude of other titles, and because one is not required to examine the further implications of such a usage. Yet wherever a reflective and systematic treatment of the concept is undertaken, guru is invariably seen either as serving merely as a starting point, or as being inadequate for a fully developed christology. This concern is expressed by most Indian Christian theologians. They believe that the concept of guru, standing alone, is not an adequate christological model; it should necessarily be complemented by the concept of *avatar*. This is primarily because most Indian theologians work with the idea that guru simply denotes teacher.

In the dialogue between Rammohan Roy and Joshua Marshman, Marshman's criticism of Roy fell along these same lines. For example, Roy writes in reply to Marshman's criticism:

> I am sorry that I cannot, without offending my conscience, agree with the Reverend Editor [Marshman] in the opinion, that "If Jesus be esteemed merely a teacher, the greater degree of honour must be given to Moses, for it was in reality his law that Jesus explained and established."[117]

In a similar fashion Sham Rao, writing on contemporary guru cults in India, saw the concept of guru as being inadequate for christology.

> We cannot, for instance, ignore the concepts of *avatara* and *guru* which have moulded the Indian religious consciousness. But we cannot use *avatara* and incarnation as interchangeable terms, nor can Christ be understood merely as a *guru*. But the concepts are relevant starting points, and need to be studied in depth by Indian Christian thinkers.[118]

Thus the concept of guru, as understood by these Christian theologians, is not a viable christological model.

3) My study clearly indicates that, even though the concept of guru is generally used as a christological model—whether it be deemed adequate or inadequate—the guru concept as it is propounded by Saiva Siddhanta has never been explored to the fullest extent. The Saivite concept is often rejected on the basis of its link to the Saivite mythologies, and the reflective tradition within Tamil Saivism is never taken into serious account. This was clearly noted in our discussion of the apologetic and theological discourses.

4) Finally, the idea of Jesus as guru is often rejected on the basis of the claim that it does not adequately explain the question of the "person" of Christ, which is explicated in the ecclesiastical creeds with Greek philosophical categories. Therefore any constructive use of "guru" in christology depends on a fresh understanding of christology that frees it from being rigidly tied to such categories as "nature" and "substance." Indian Christian theologians have, for the most part, operated with a christology that was handed over to them by the missionaries, who saw the christological task as manipulating the existing Hindu thought-forms to express the unchanging and

eternal truths concerning Jesus the Christ. The New Testament christologies and the creedal expressions of the church were seen as "static," which could only be "dressed up" in the local idiom and thought-patterns. They were not allowed to enter into a relationship with Hindu concepts in a way that would mutually influence Hindu and Christian ideas. I maintain that any creative use of guru involves a two-way traffic between the concept of guru in Saiva Siddhanta and the traditional christology, each informing and shaping the other. As Samartha rightly points out:

> The function of Christology now is not to start a frantic search for an alternative "substance," whether home-made or imported from else-where, in order once again to understand Christ's nature. It is, rather, to seek an answer to the question: What is the reality that we encounter in Jesus Christ, the crucified and risen Lord? It is to understand and explain the significance of the cluster of events centering around the person and work of Christ.[119]

Thus the task of christology is not to search for an apt vocabulary within the Indian religious tradition to translate the concepts and ideas surrounding the traditional and creedal formulations of significance of Jesus the Christ. Rather, it is to find ways to get at the significance of Jesus the Christ in and through the religious thought of India.

CHAPTER 4

THE CRUCIFIED GURU

I began this inquiry by locating the Saiva concept of guru within its historical and theological contexts. This was followed by an analysis of the various ways in which religious thinkers in India have and have not used the guru concept christologically. That investigation revealed that Saiva Siddhanta's concept of guru has never been explored to the fullest extent, particularly with an eye to the possibilities it holds for christological construction. In this chapter I outline how one can employ the Saiva concept of guru to explain the significance of Jesus the Christ. What does it mean to say that Jesus is the guru, when guru is understood within the Saiva Siddhanta tradition? This chapter attempts an answer to this question.

SOME METHODOLOGICAL CONSIDERATIONS

The nature of any portrait of Jesus is dependent on the context in which it is painted. The context for this portrait is the dialogue between Christian understandings of Jesus the Christ and the Saiva Siddhanta concept of guru. This context necessitates the use of terms and concepts that belong to the Saivite tradition, and which may be foreign to the language of the New Testament. At such points it will be possible to justify my use of such concepts on the basis of the historical details of the life of Jesus. In this portrait of Jesus as guru, I limit myself to the guru concept as it is developed and explicated within the more reflective and systematic traditions of Tamil Saivism. For that reason I do not employ the popular and unreflective notions of guru.

Further, my portrait of Jesus aims to offer a fresh understanding of the person and work of Jesus the Christ also to Christians, especially those in Tamilnadu. This portrait of Jesus involves many historical and theological questions. One may ask whether I am faithful to the theological and christological heritage of the Christian community. In the history of Christianity several and varied metaphorical names and titles have been used to explicate the significance of Jesus. However, I am not proposing simply to make the title "guru" one among many titles such as "Son of God," "Lord," "Messiah," and so on. Rather I use "guru" to function as the overriding and guiding model around which my vision of Jesus is organized. It may or may not incorporate within itself the concerns implied in the other titles. For example, the use of "guru" necessarily implies the rejection of the title *avatar,* when "guru" is understood within the Saiva Siddhanta tradition. At the same time, I would argue that "guru" is comprehensive enough to accommodate the various theological and soteriological concerns implied in *avatar.*

When one attempts to present a picture of Jesus and his significance, one needs to be aware of the various historical questions involved in such a project. Is the figure of Jesus a historical human being or merely the fancy of a group of people who called themselves his disciples? As far as modern historical study is concerned, most scholars agree that there lived a human being called Jesus in the biblical land of Galilee during the early years of the first century C.E. However, there are considerable differences of opinion concerning the details of his life. What events in the life of Jesus, as recorded in the early Christian writings, are historical and factual? What are Jesus' authentic sayings and teachings? These are questions that involve lengthy, extensive, and complex arguments and debate if one were to seek to answer them. I do not go into these debates here.

However, modern critical study of the documents of the early church has shown that it is difficult, even impossible, to reconstruct a biography of Jesus that will satisfy the demands of the historical and critical mind.[1] At most we can say that Jesus was a teacher, a healer, and an itinerant preacher who was put to death by crucifixion during the reign of Pontius Pilate, the Roman governor at Jerusalem, around the year 29 C.E. Yet we do have reasonable access to a coherent picture of Jesus as seen through the eyes of the early Christian community that had come to acknowledge him as having ultimate and decisive significance for one's view of and orientation for human life. It is this picture or "perspectival image"[2] that we are concerned with in this chapter as I attempt to reconstruct a portrait of Jesus applying the title "guru" to him. I am aware that the New Testament picture of Jesus is informed and shaped by the events surrounding the resurrection of Jesus. Yet I will first attempt a portrait without any specific reference to the resurrection, and only later consider its particular ramifications.

Thus what I am doing here is retelling the story of Jesus and explicating his significance with the help of the title "guru." In retelling the story I accommodate, as far as possible, the questions of historicity. I take account of the modern historical scholarship of the New Testament and the history of early Christianity. Since my retelling of the story is an exercise in christological story-telling rather than biography, my overall emphasis is on the theological and soteriological significance of Jesus, seen through the paradigm of "guru."

My portrayal of Jesus as the guru is not a fully and extensively developed christology; it aims to fulfill only three tasks. First, it gives us a picture of Jesus that is sufficient provisionally to answer the question of who Jesus is and what his significance will be if one ascribes the title "guru" to him. Second, my portrait enables us to discover the points at which the concept of guru and the significance of Jesus converge, and where they diverge. This will provide us a way to explicate the problems and possibilities in the use of "guru" as a title for Christ. Third, it gives directions for how one might develop a full-fledged christology with "guru" as the organizing paradigm.

JESUS THE GURU

What does it mean to say "Jesus is the guru"? To begin, we need to mention the term's correlative, *sisya* (disciple). It means that guru can be understood only in relation to disciple. There can be no guru without a disciple, nor can there be a disciple without a guru. As Irudhayaraj writes:

A guru is guru because a sisya sits at his feet. The loving link between these two is what is most fundamental in the guru-idea. In the absence of this relationship, a wandering Sadhu, a Sannyasi of great renunciation, or a Rsi in contemplation in his forest retreat, cannot be considered a guru.[3]

Thus it is the relationship between the guru and the disciples that makes the guruship of a guru real. Therefore my exposition of the guruship of Jesus may well begin with the encounter between Jesus and his disciples.

Interestingly, the gospel according to Mark, most probably the earliest of the four Gospels in the New Testament, begins the story of Jesus with John the Baptizer's recognition and announcement of the guruship of Jesus.

He [John] proclaimed, "The one who is more powerful than I is coming after me; I am not worthy to stoop down and untie the thong of his sandals. I have baptized you with water; but he will baptize you with the Holy Spirit." (Mark 1:7-8)

The Fourth Gospel, the latest of the four, presents John as pointing to Jesus and recommending him as guru to a few of his own disciples.[4] These disciples recognized the guruship of Jesus and followed him to the place where he stayed and became his disciples. The Gospels go on to narrate several incidents in which Jesus called several other disciples, who then followed him. As the story of Jesus' early ministry unfolds, it is a story not only of the individual Jesus, but of Jesus and his disciples. Jesus emerges as a guru with his disciples, who recognize and accept him as such.

What was the nature of the relationship that came about between the guru Jesus and his disciples? Mark writes:

He [Jesus] went up the mountain and called to him those whom he wanted, and they came to him. And he appointed twelve, whom he also named apostles, to be with him, and to be sent out to proclaim the message, and to have authority to cast out demons. (Mark 3:13-15)

The relationship between Jesus and his disciples entails two aspects. First, it involves a community of proximity ("to be with him"), of affection and love for one another, and of interdependence. Second, the relationship implies a commission, a task or a vocation "to be sent out to proclaim the message . . . to cast out demons." All four Gospels portray these two aspects of the guru-sisya relationship in their narration of the various incidents in the life of Jesus and his disciples. For example, the calming of the stormy sea by Jesus portrays the dependence of the disciples on their guru (Mark 4:35ff.).[5] Similarly, the agony and the struggle of Jesus in the garden of Gethsemane present Jesus as asking his disciples to sustain him with their prayers (Mark 14:32ff.; Matt. 26:36ff.; Luke 22:40ff.). Jesus often articulates his vocation as one of being sent by God to preach the kingdom of God; he in turn sends his disciples to preach (Mark 1:38 and 6:7ff.). Thus the community of the guru and the disciples is brought into a focus with a common commission to preach. Strength enough to fulfill the commission comes from the sustaining character of the community that exists between the guru and the disciples.

Once the relationship between the guru and the disciples is established, the disciples tend to portray the guruship of Jesus as being preexistent to, and independent of, their recognition of him as a guru. This is what I find in the early chapters of the Gospels according to Matthew, Luke, and John. The overwhelming and compelling presence of the guru demands such a move. Matthew traces the origins of Jesus to Abraham, the progenitor of the people of Israel. His stories concerning the miraculous birth of Jesus portray the same concern to establish the guruship of Jesus independent of the disciples (Matthew 1 and 2). In addition to the stories about Jesus' miraculous birth, Luke narrates a story about Jesus as a boy of twelve playing the role of guru in his discussion with the rabbis in the Temple at Jerusalem (Luke 2:46). The author of the Fourth Gospel goes even further to designate Jesus as being present in the universe as Logos long before his appearance on earth as a human being (John 1:1-18). The Johannine Logos was, in the words of Sri Parananda, the "Informer of the Universe" or the "Teacher of the Universe" before he took on human flesh in Jesus the guru.[6] Moreover, the Gospels present the stories about the call of the disciples as though the disciples had only a passive and submissive role to play, even though they were actively involved in recognizing Jesus as the guru and responding to his call. Mark writes:

> As Jesus passed along the Sea of Galilee, he saw Simon and his brother Andrew casting a net into the sea—for they were fishermen. And Jesus said to them, "Follow me and I will make you fish for people." And immediately they left their nets and followed him. (Mark 1:16-18)

The disciples' response looks almost magical. Yet we should note that these stories were written after the disciples had been convinced of the guruship of Jesus and had come to offer their complete loyalty to him.

Having noted the tendency on the part of the disciples to describe the guruship of Jesus as independent of their response, let us look at the ministry of Jesus in the matrix of the guru-sisya relation. Our examination of the guru concept in Saiva Siddhanta noted that the guru, once recognized as guru, *functions* as God to the disciples. Note here that the application of the title "guru" to Jesus carries with it the implication that Jesus is *not* an *avatar* (incarnation). This means that one is not equating the identity of Jesus with God. Incarnational language in its mythical form gets trapped repeatedly in a discussion about the "stuff" of which Jesus is made. A vision of Jesus as the guru does not raise the question of the constitution of Jesus' personality. He is a human being; yet the disciples see him functioning as God to them in what he does and teaches. Thus the guru's presence makes God's presence real to the disciples.

At a crucial moment in the ministry of Jesus, he asks his disciples what they think about him. Peter answers, "You are the Messiah, the Son of the living God" (Matt. 16:16). Here is the recognition that Jesus' presence should be conceived in relation to God's presence among them. In the Fourth Gospel the functional presence of God in Jesus is expressed through the professed sayings of Jesus. When Philip asks Jesus to show them the Father (God), Jesus answers thus:

> Have I been with you all this time, Philip, and you still do not know me? Whoever has seen me has seen the Father. How can you say, "Show us the Father"? Do you not believe that I am in the Father and the Father is in me? . . . Believe me that I am in the Father and the

Father is in me; but if you do not, then believe me because of the works themselves. (John 14:9-11)

Noteworthy here is the fact that Jesus functions as God to the disciples through the "works" that Jesus does and not from who Jesus is. In the same passage Jesus refers to his words as functioning as God's word to the disciples. In everything that the guru does, both the words and the works, Jesus functions as God to the disciples.

What does guru Jesus do? First, Jesus teaches. As George M. Soares-Prabhu, a Roman Catholic theologian in India, writes:

All three synoptics feature "teaching" as a prominent element in the ministry of Jesus. It is mentioned conspicuously by Matthew in his strategically placed summaries of the Galilean ministry of Jesus, which tell us how he "went around Galilee, *teaching* in their synagogue, *preaching* the good news of the kingdom, and healing every disease and every infirmity" (Mt. 4,23; 9,35; 11,1). Mark too likes to show Jesus teaching great crowds on the shores of the lake of Gennasereth (Mk. 2,13; 4,1; 6,34); and Luke has frequent reference to Jesus teaching in synagogues (Lk. 4,15; 4,31; 6,6; 13,10) or in the Temple (Lk. 19,47; 20,1; 21,37).[7]

Moreover, there are several occasions in the Gospel stories where Jesus is addressed as teacher by both his disciples and others.[8]

The guruship of Jesus is not limited to the fact that he teaches; it is determined by both the content and the method of teaching that a guru adopts. Therefore we need to look at the content of Jesus' teachings as well as the nature and method of his teaching ministry. Let us begin with the nature of his teaching. The first aspect of his teaching is its public character. Though Jesus confided privately to his chosen disciples some of the deeper meanings of his teaching, he was a guru whose teaching was open to all classes of people, disciples or otherwise (Mark 4:10ff.). As Soares-Prabhu remarks:

This educational project [of Jesus] is, according to the Synoptic tradition a public project. The teaching of Jesus is not academic teaching restricted to the members of a scribal school trained in the Law . . . nor is it a secret religious teaching given only to a select group of initiates who have been admitted into "the covenant of grace."[9]

Jesus the guru, though fully recognized and accepted as guru only by his disciples, addresses his teaching to all people—men, women, and children alike.[10] Soares-Prabhu is right in calling it "a non-elitist pedagogy."

Second, Jesus taught with authority. Invariably the initial reaction of those who heard him was amazement at his authority. In Mark 1:22 we read, "They were astounded at his teaching, for he taught them as one having authority, and not as the scribes." His authority rested neither on the basis of his belonging to a *guruparamparai* (succession of gurus), nor on his belonging to an elite class within society. Jesus' authority was dependent on his unique relationship to God and his own identification with those whom he taught.[11] Moreover, his authority was not that which demanded an unquestioning and absolute obedience from the disciple. His power was one of persuasion and loving invitation. As Irudhayaraj writes:

> A guru is not a mother feeding her child, nor a master ordering his servant, nor a normal man leading a blind man. The relation between guru and sisya is rather like that of light and the eye, or call and the response. The guru belongs inwardly to the process of spiritual realization as light to the act of seeing.[12]

Third, Jesus' teaching was one of enacted words. His teaching was accompanied by his own acts, which symbolized that teaching and made it concrete. For example, he washed the feet of his disciples and taught them the priority of love for and humble service to one another (John 13:1-15). Recording this incident, the author of the Fourth Gospel ends the story thus:

> After he [Jesus] had washed their feet . . . he said to them, "Do you know what I have done to you? You call me Teacher and Lord—and you are right, for that is what I am. So if I, your Lord and Teacher, have washed your feet, you also ought to wash one another's feet."
> (John 13:12-14)

Moreover, the teaching of Jesus did not aim to increase the amount of knowledge stored in the minds of the disciples; it aimed at enabling the disciples to act out what he taught. The well-known parable of the good Samaritan ends with Jesus' injunction, "Go and do likewise" (Luke 10:37). At the end of the collection of his teachings traditionally known as the Sermon on the Mount, Jesus says:

> Not everyone who says to me, "Lord, Lord," will enter the kingdom of heaven, but only the one who *does* the will of my Father in heaven. . . .
> Everyone then who hears these words of mine and *acts* on them will be like a wise man who built his house on rock.
>
> (Matt. 7:21, 24, italics added)

As Soares-Prabhu rightly calls it, the teaching of Jesus was a praxis-oriented pedagogy.[13]

What was the content of the teachings of Jesus? According to Saiva Siddhanta, every guru teaches his disciples the three basic verities of religious life, namely, *pati* (God), *pasu* (soul), and *pasam* (bondage). Jesus did teach about these three. He summed them up in a phrase that was characteristic of his teaching: the reign of God. Introducing the early ministry of Jesus, Mark records, "Jesus came to Galilee, proclaiming the good news of God, and saying, 'The time is fulfilled, and the kingdom of God has come near; repent, and believe in the good news'" (Mark 1:14-15).

The reign of God in the teachings of Jesus presents us a vision of God as the Creator and Lord of the universe who demands a radical obedience from humans. This is why the teaching of Jesus that announces the coming of the reign is always accompanied by a call to repent and obey. God is one who brings judgment on all that is humanity's own creation. The reign is that which irrupts into history and brings God's judgment on human history and on human society with all its structures. Jesus' proclamation of the Jubilee year at the synagogue at Nazareth epitomizes this judgmental aspect of God's reign (Luke 4:16ff.), as do several parables in the teachings of Jesus (for example, see Matt. 13:24ff., 47ff., and 25:31ff.). The author of the Fourth Gospel is much more explicit in his presentation of the idea of the judgment of God (John 3:17-21). This emphasis on God's otherness and judgment is coupled with an equal emphasis on the grace and mercy of God. God is likened to a "father" who accepts even the son "who has devoured your property with prostitutes" (Luke 15:30).[14] God is one who forgives and accepts the sinner while judging and condemning sin. Jesus' own identification with the marginalized people in society, such as the tax-gatherers and harlots, signifies this gracious aspect of God.

The concept of the reign of God symbolizes also a vision of human community and its individual members. Humans, who are under the judgment and mercy of God, are called upon to love and care for one another, as children of the same God. A new order of relationships is made possible by the coming of the reign. This new order is defined by justice to all and peace or reconciliation with one another. For example, Jesus began his ministry by proclaiming at Nazareth his manifesto:

> The Spirit of the Lord is upon me,
>   because he has anointed me
>   to bring good news to the poor.
> He has sent me to proclaim release to captives
>   and recovery of sight to the blind,
>   to let the oppressed go free,
>   to proclaim the year of the Lord's favor. (Luke 4:18)

The announcement of the reign of God helps the disciples see what the problem of the human condition is. What is *pasam* (bondage)? Humans refuse to be themselves. They refuse to be "under" God and "with" others. In other words, humans fail to accept divine sovereignty (which challenges them as both judgment and mercy) and human solidarity (which involves both justice and peace). The guru's proclamation of the reign of God liberates the disciples to be themselves, to be "under" God and to be "with" others. Jesus summarized his teaching in these words: "The Lord our God, the Lord is one; you shall love the Lord your God with all your heart, and with all your soul. . . . You shall love your neighbor as yourself" (Mark 12:29-31).

A guru's powerful appeal is not limited to his words alone. As Saiva Siddhanta portrays, the guru effects changes in the lives of the disciples by his touch and by his look. The healing ministry of Jesus illustrates this aspect of the guru's function.[15] In Mark 5:25ff., we read about a woman who had a flow of blood for twelve years; she was healed of her disease by touching the garment of Jesus. Jesus touches the lepers, the blind, and the demon-possessed, and they receive healing.[16] In narrating the story of Peter's denial of Jesus, Luke ends the story by saying, "The Lord [Jesus] turned and looked at Peter. Then Peter remembered the word of the Lord. . . . And he went out and wept bitterly" (Luke 22:61f.). Thus we see in Jesus a guru who by his touch and look appeals to the hearts and minds of his disciples, bringing healing and wholeness.

One of the ways in which the relationship between the guru and the disciple is defined is through the idea of *diksa* (initiatory rites). In the life and ministry of Jesus the guru, two such rites emerge: Baptism and Eucharist. They are not, however, similar to the *diksa* in Saiva Siddhanta, for two reasons. First, whether Jesus himself administered baptism to his followers is a debatable question.[17] And the second rite, the Eucharist, took a definite shape only at the end of Jesus' ministry, though one might consider all the communal meals in which Jesus participated as eucharistic meals. Second, these two *diksas* assume their full symbolic character only after the physical presence of the guru is removed from the disciples. These rites are discussed again later in this chapter.

What I have presented up to this point is a picture of Jesus the guru in the context of his relationship to his disciples, and in terms of what he taught and did. As the story unfolds further, we see that the guru's influence was not limited to the circle of his disciples, but rather that it had far-reaching consequences in the society in which they lived. Again, this was primarily due to the public character of Jesus' teachings and actions. The reign of God, which was a new community of peace and justice embodied in the life and ministry of Jesus and his disciples, created a situation of conflict with the existing religious and sociopolitical structures of Jesus' day. The community of Jesus and his disciples was seen as a threat to the existing order by both religious and political leaders. This community questioned the authority embedded in religious institutions such as the temple and the synagogue, and in the political offices of the Roman rulers.[18] This conflict ultimately led to the arrest of Jesus and his death on the cross as a religious and political criminal. The guru was put to death.

What did this mean for the community of disciples? Two implications come to mind: First, Jesus' death on the cross came as a logical climax and the natural consequence of his ministry. In other words, what Jesus taught and did could not but lead to such a resolution, tragic though it was, of the conflict. Second, the cross came as the supreme enactment of all that Jesus stood for. The guru who advocated self-sacrifice was himself the embodiment of self-sacrifice on the cross. He was thoroughly himself on the cross—under God and with others, accepting divine sovereignty and human solidarity in pain, suffering, and death.

If the story of guru Jesus had ended with his death on the cross, it would have remained a story of the past. It would have been a remembered story but not a relevant story for humanity today. It would have meant nothing, except that once there was a guru who lived and met a tragic death. At best one might see merit in his teachings and attempt to follow them. Yet the story of Jesus the guru did not stop with his tragic death on the cross. It was followed by a nexus of events known as Resurrection, Ascension, and Pentecost. These events effected a dramatic change in the understanding of the guruship of Jesus. Before we go into these changes in the vision of Jesus, a few methodological issues demand our attention.

First, I treat the complex of events called Resurrection, Ascension, and Pentecost as a unified whole and not as separate events. I do so because these events are of a historical character different from, for example, the death of Jesus. In these events one can talk about what happened to the disciples, but not about what happened to Jesus himself, because with his death Jesus ceases to be a historical figure by our understanding of that term. By taking these events together as a whole, I am indicating my emphasis on the changes in the vision of Jesus as guru. Further, the Gospels themselves present these events as a continuum. In his introduction to the Acts of the Apostles, Luke spells out the continuity that is involved (Acts 1:1ff.). John goes even further, depicting all three together as happening on the same day (John 20:1ff.). The risen Jesus ascends and comes back to the disciples to grant them the Holy Spirit.

The historicity of these events as such is not the primary concern here. Did Jesus come out of the grave? Did he physically ascend into heaven? How did the Spirit descend on the disciples? These questions can be addressed elsewhere.[19] The questions I want to ask are, What is the picture of Jesus the guru that emerges out of this complex of events? Do these events make any difference in the vision of Jesus as guru? Let me mention some of the differences that this nexus of events makes in the guruship of Jesus.

First, the presence of the guru among his disciples was understood in an entirely different manner. Jesus the guru was no longer available to the disciples as a physical presence among them. Yet he was very much present among them as the Spirit of Jesus, the Holy Spirit. They were convinced that he was alive (though not in a normal physical manner, because he was supposed to have entered through closed doors) and was present as a risen guru. At the same time, the "spiritual" guru who was accessible to them was not anyone different from the human guru in character. It was the same Jesus (with scars in his hands, his feet, and his sides) who was present to them in the risen and living guru. It is interesting to see how the discourse about Jesus as teacher shifts at that point to a discussion of the Holy Spirit as teacher. Jesus' farewell discourse, as narrated in the Fourth Gospel, contains repeated references to the Holy Spirit as the teacher of truth, not contradicting the human guru but rather enhancing and furthering the role of the human guru Jesus. Jesus says:

> I still have many things to say to you, but you cannot bear them now. When the Spirit of truth comes, he will guide you into all the truth; for he will not speak on his own, but will speak whatever he hears. . . . He will glorify me, because he will take what is mine and declare it to you. (John 16:12-14)

Second, the death of Jesus on the cross was seen in a new light. No longer was it the tragic and unfortunate death of a guru. The cross became the supreme and climactic point at which the guru was to be seen as being fully himself—the embodiment of what he taught and did. It became a symbol of the guru's victory over sin and death. By his powerlessness on the cross, the guru gives a fresh and novel understanding of wherein lay true power—the power of love and self-sacrifice. On the cross the guru is no longer seen as a mere pointer to the way of liberated existence, but he himself can now be seen as "the way, the truth and the life." There the reign of God is at its fullest manifestation—a reign of love and justice and of God's judgment and mercy. It is no longer the teacher-guru who dominates the scene, but the victim-guru, the dying guru, the crucified guru who appears as the guru par excellence.

Third, the nexus of events I am referring to here raised the status of the guru from a local to a universal plane. Jesus was no longer the local guru of first-century Galilee but a guru for all ages and all people. He was no longer confined to the limitations of space and time. He was raised to a level where he could demand adoration and loyalty from all peoples in all places. This was why the author of the Fourth Gospel could open his narrative with the idea of Logos, the universal creative principle of God, taking flesh in the human Jesus (John 1:1-18). Similarly Paul could write concerning the guru:

> He is the image of the invisible God, the firstborn of all creation; for in him all things in heaven and on earth were created, things visible and invisible. . . . He himself is before all things, and in him all things hold together. (Col. 1:15-17)

What is the kind of universality that we are ascribing to Jesus here? We need to recall the correlative character of the ideas of guru and disciple. A guru gains his significance, if any at all, only in the context of the guru-sisya relation. The salvific efficacy of a guru is not an objective reality as such; rather, it is dependent on the imaginative vision of those who come to recognize him as a guru. This is one of the reasons why Saiva Siddhanta believes in a multiplicity of gurus. Even when the disciples of Jesus raise him to a level of universality on the basis of the events linked to his resurrection, it is they who do so; the universal significance of Jesus is dependent on their vision. Thus the universal significance of Jesus is not an objective empirical reality that can be verified and established through a process of collecting empirical evidences. It is the product of the imaginative vision of the disciples, however much the nexus of events surrounding the resurrection might have contributed to it. The difficulty one faces in finding out what exactly happened to Jesus in this nexus of events reinforces the claim that it is the imaginative vision of the disciples that is determinative in construing the universal significance of Jesus.

Fourth, we note the difference in the disciples' understanding of Jesus' relation to God. Earlier in my discussion of the ministry of Jesus, I noted how the disciples came to see him functioning as God to them. With the belief in the resurrection of the guru the idea of divine presence in what the guru taught and did was reinforced. The resurrection of the guru was seen as the divine vindication of what Jesus stood for. This is why the early Christians referred to Jesus' resurrection not as Jesus himself rising from the dead, but rather as God raising Jesus from the dead and appointing him guru for all. Peter's sermon in the book of Acts goes thus: "This man, handed over to you according to the definite plan and foreknowledge of God, you crucified and killed. . . . But God raised him up" (Acts 2:23-24). In one of the earliest accounts of the resurrection of Jesus, Paul refers to Jesus' resurrection in the same manner: "He [Jesus] was buried, . . . he was raised on the third day in accordance with the scriptures" (1 Cor. 15:4).

Fifth, the two initiatory rites recommended by the guru, Baptism and Eucharist, take on a distinctive character. They are no longer rites or symbolic acts that are performed by the guru on the disciples. Because of the physical absence of the guru, these rites become community acts, which the disciples of Jesus perform and participate in as a community. These rites become communal acts for the mutual edification of the members of the new community of disciples. They are no longer acts performed by an individual guru on an individual disciple; instead, their communal aspect is highlighted.

Sixth, there is a dramatic change in the understanding of discipleship. While the guru is physically present, a disciple may have the temptation to be a passive recipient of the guru's instruction. With the physical absence of the guru, discipleship has to be seen in much more active terms. The disciples become the chief actors in the context of the guru-sisya relationship. The guru's presence hereafter can only be maintained by the life of the community of disciples. Recording the incidents in the last few days of Jesus' life, the author of the Fourth Gospel puts into the mouth of Jesus the following words: "I give you a new commandment, that you love one another. Just as I have loved you, you also should love one another. By this everyone will know that you are my disciples, if you have love for one another" (John 13:34-35). It is the community of disciples who bear witness to the presence of the guru among them. Theologian Hans Frei writes, "The church is both the witness to that presence and the public and communal form the indirect presence of Christ now takes, in contrast to his direct presence in his earthly days."[20]

To sum up this portrait of Jesus as guru, several remarks can be made. First, when I say "Jesus is guru," I am not merely referring to an individual historical guru of first-century Galilee, but to an image of a "risen" guru Jesus that is informed and shaped by the human Jesus who taught, healed, and was crucified. His significance as one who unfolds the mystery of the reign of God and as one who reveals *pati, pasu,* and *pasam,* is dependent, from beginning to end, on the fact that his disciples, ancient and modern, have envisioned him as having such significance. Thus it is the spirit of Jesus or the Holy Spirit who enables the disciples to enter into the new order of relationships in which humans see themselves as being "under" God and "with" others. Any human being who comes to owe allegiance and loyalty to this guru sees himself or herself as under the judgment and mercy of God and empowered to live in a community of justice and peace. In the life of such a disciple, the cross becomes the central symbol of the nature and mode of discipleship. As Jesus himself said:

> If any want to become my followers, let them deny themselves and take up their cross and follow me. For those who want to save their life will lose it, and those who lose their life for my sake, and for the sake of the gospel, will save it. (Mark 8:34-35)

Second, we need to note the points at which this portrait of Jesus the guru differs from the Saivite vision of the guru. Both the content and the method of the teachings of Jesus have certain peculiar features. His teachings have a public character that is alien to the guru concept in Saiva Siddhanta. They are also devoid of any authoritarian overtones. Even though the idea of the reign of God encompasses the three main categories—God, soul, and bondage—it is different in content from the Saivite explication of these categories. Also to be noted is the difference between the idea of *diksas* in Saiva Siddhanta and the two sacraments, Baptism and Eucharist. Whereas Christian discipleship is expressed in and through a community of disciples who gather around the eucharistic table and go out into the world as Christ's disciples, Saivite discipleship is founded on a one-to-one relationship between the guru and the disciple. Furthermore, the crucifixion and the nexus of events surrounding the resurrection of Jesus give a distinctive character to the vision of Jesus as guru, a character that is foreign to the guru concept in Saivism. For example, the resurrection of Jesus has elevated the status of the guru to a universal plane, whereas in Saiva Siddhanta the guru is primarily understood as local and as an individual. How far can these differences be accommodated within the concept of guru? This question is addressed next.

CHAPTER 5

POSSIBILITIES AND PROBLEMS

My attempt to explore the possibilities of the christological use of the concept of guru in Saiva Siddhanta began by locating the guru concept within the historical and philosophical matrix of Saiva Siddhanta. This examination was followed by a survey of the various ways in which both Christian and non-Christian thinkers in India had used "guru" as a christological title. We saw that, in most cases, the guru concept was rejected as being christologically inadequate for one of two reasons. On the one hand, Christian theologians in India did not fully appreciate the concept of guru as it was presented in the mature and reflective traditions within Saiva Siddhanta. Therefore their rejection of guru was mainly dependent on the popular and less reflective understanding of the guru concept. On the other hand, they worked with a kind of christological positivism that envisioned the christological task as a "translation" of scriptural and creedal statements, and hence it inhibited them from a creative use of the concept of guru. Having noted this historical antecedent, I sketched out a portrait of Jesus and his significance by applying the title "guru" to him.

Now the task before us is to explore the possibilities and problems involved in the christological use of guru. In this exploration we will be guided by several considerations. First is to maintain a two-way movement between the Saiva Siddhanta concept of guru and the christological portrait of Jesus. Our recognition of the interconnectedness of humanity impels us to respect the integrity of each religious tradition. Such a respect for the other demands that we enter into a dialogue with, and promote exchange between, various religious traditions as equal partners with a sense of mutuality. Therefore a two-way movement is necessary. I maintain the two-way movement in the following way. The distinctive features of the concept of guru are brought in to influence and shape my explication of the significance of Jesus. For example, I use the idea of multiplicity of gurus to challenge the traditional understanding of the finality of Christ. In a similar fashion, the elements peculiar to my portrait of Jesus function as correctives to the Saiva Siddhanta understanding of guru. To cite an example, the vision of a crucified guru offers a critique of and a corrective to the possible authoritarian portrayal of guru.

Another consideration is to initiate a dialogue between the various christologies that are available in today's world. The kind of globalization that I mentioned at the beginning demands that christologians from different parts of the world engage in conversation and mutual enrichment. My examination of the christological possibilities will, it is hoped, enable and enhance such a dialogue.

Further, though the concept of guru is found in both the reflective and popular writings in the Saiva Siddhanta tradition, I give priority to the former because christology is mainly a reflective and conceptual discipline.[1] Earlier we saw how the early Christian missionaries were preoccupied with criticizing popular notions of guru, and how this enabled them to establish, easily and uncritically, the superiority of Jesus the Christ over all the other gurus. I deliberately avoid such an "apologetic" posture since my main concern is to initiate a dialogue between Christians and Saivites in Tamilnadu. These considerations, then, determine the direction of my assessment of the possibilities and problems in guru christology.

This chapter seeks to address the following questions: Does the concept of guru adequately convey the decisive significance of the confession of Jesus as the Christ? Is it relevant to the context of Tamilnadu, India? Does it offer any creative possibilities for a meaningful and fruitful human existence today? Does it offer opportunities for a global conversation on christological concerns?

CONTEXTUALIZATION AND GLOBALIZATION: POSSIBILITIES AND PROBLEMS

The concept of guru belongs to the common vocabulary of the people of Tamilnadu, whom I am attempting to address. One can find the term "guru" (in its transliterated form) in all the principal languages in South India. This means that when one applies the term guru to Jesus, such christological talk is intelligible and credible to the South Indian people. Particularly because the Saivites in Tamilnadu have a well-developed notion of guru, my christology will be understandable to them. It has great potential for communicating the christological concern—the decisive significance of Jesus—to the listener. Though guru can denote any secular teacher or professor, it has definite theological and soteriological implications when employed in religious discourse. Since the concept of guru has been constructed in the context of the concepts of God, the world, and the human—very similar to any christological articulation—it has this potential. Because of this immediate intelligibility, guru christology is relevant for Tamilnadu.

Given the fact that guru christology is intelligible, one should further ask whether it adequately communicates the significance of Jesus as it has been explicated in the Christian tradition. My answer cannot be straightforward. Since the explication of the significance of Jesus has developed through the centuries inside Jewish, Greek, Roman, and other Western systems of thought, it can have certain peculiarities that may not belong to the concept of guru that has taken shape in the history of Indian religious and philosophical discourse. Moreover, the vision of the significance of Jesus is linked with certain historical peculiarities due to its relation to a historically unique individual Jesus and the events surrounding him. Therefore talk about the significance of Jesus will have certain distinctive features that may be foreign to the concept of guru. For example, the idea of a crucified and risen guru is alien to Saiva Siddhanta. Therefore one cannot assume that the concept of guru adequately presents all christological concerns from the outset. Yet it can accommodate the distinctive christological variations because of its immediate intelligibility. In short, the idea of a *crucified* and *risen* guru may be foreign to Saiva Siddhanta; but since *guru* is basically understandable, this idea is not utterly incomprehensible or beyond the horizon of understanding of the Saivites.

The concept of guru is intelligible not only to Saivites but also to Christians in Tamilnadu. I noted in chapter 3 that the Tamil Christian poets frequently applied this title to Jesus, and therefore the idea of

Jesus as guru is already present in the Tamil Christian mind. Thus the idea of guru is intelligible and understandable both to Saivites and to Christians in Tamilnadu. As Tiliander, a Christian missionary from Sweden who did a study of Christian and Hindu terminology in Tamilnadu, writes: "The word Sarguru [true guru] is not only bound to attract the attention of Hindus when Christ is presented under that name, it touches also the hearts of Christians."[2] Thus guru christology can open the doors for a fruitful and sustained dialogue between Christians and Saivites in Tamilnadu.

While I maintain that guru christology is intelligible to both Saivites and Christians in Tamilnadu, I need also to mention that the concept of guru is not utterly foreign to the West. The word "guru" has become well known in the English language, and one finds it quite regularly in modern-day writings in English. Often it means "expert" or "specialist" in Western secular usage. The arrival as well of several popular Hindu gurus in Western countries, beginning from 1960 onward, helped people in the West become well acquainted with the word. Whatever meanings and connotations the West gives to the concept of guru, it is a familiar idea, and hence understandable and intelligible, most of the world over today.

One of the strengths of the concept of guru is that it transfers the significance of Jesus to a level of ultimacy and decisiveness. In my examination of the concept of guru in Saiva Siddhanta, I mentioned that guru gains its meaning in the context of the three eternal verities: God (pati), soul (pasu), and bondage (pasam). These three categories are metaphysical in the sense that they map out the ultimate context of human existence. Thus guru is seen as the one who enables the soul to be freed from the threefold bondage, to be united with Sivam. Therefore when the title "guru" is ascribed to Jesus, he is bound to be seen in the light of a vision of the ultimate context of life.

The point I am making is well illustrated by examining the level of discourse to which some of the traditional titles of Jesus relate. For example, when one applies the title "Son of God" to Jesus in the Tamil Saivite context, the discourse is immediately transferred to a popular level because only in the Saivite mythologies does one come across the idea of Son of God. Siva is said to have two sons, Murugan (sometimes referred to as Subramaniyan) and Ganesh (otherwise called Pillaiyar). So when one refers to Jesus as the Son of God, the

Saivite mind immediately links it to the mythological discourse within the tradition. Even qualifications such as "only son" or "begotten not made" cannot transfer the christological discourse from the popular to the reflective level. On the other hand, the concept of guru links the discourse to the reflective tradition within Tamil Saivism and enables my articulation of the ultimate and decisive character of Jesus' significance.

Having noted that the use of "guru" as a christological title transfers christological articulation to a reflective and metaphysical level, we need to ask to what metaphysical vision it points or is based on. Metaphysics can be defined as the task of explaining the ultimate context of human life and experience through an imaginative construction of concepts, symbols, and images. Anthropologist Clifford Geertz notes that humans, as "symbolizing, conceptualizing, meaning-seeking" animals, are driven "to make sense out of experience, to give it form and order," and this drive is "as real and as pressing as the more familiar biological needs."[3] Thus humans come up with metaphysics, or "world views." The essential point here is not whether the vision corresponds to what actually exists, but rather whether it enables humans to understand, explain, and bring into a coherent whole the various differing dimensions and levels of human experience. Most often, however, these visions are presented as having a one-to-one correspondence with the actual state of affairs. This is so mainly because humans need to make their visions of the ultimate context emotionally acceptable and thus "provide orientation for an organism which cannot live in a world it is unable to understand."[4] According to Geertz,

> Their [humans'] world view is their picture of the way things in sheer actuality are, their concept of nature, of self, of society. It contains their most comprehensive ideas of order. . . . The ethos is made intellectually reasonable by being shown to represent a way of life implied by the actual state of affairs which the world view describes, and the world view is made emotionally acceptable by being presented as an image of an actual state of affairs of which such a way of life is an authentic expression.[5]

There is a particular world view, or vision, of the ultimate context of human existence which informs and shapes the idea of guru in

Saiva Siddhanta. As I mentioned earlier, this vision of the ultimate context is defined by the three eternal categories, God, soul, and bondage. In addition to these three, there is an underlying assumption that determines all of them, namely, the belief in *karma-samsara* (human actions leading to repeated births). In this way the Saiva Siddhanta vision of the ultimate context is apparently different from those metaphysical foundations which have informed christology through the ages.

I should acknowledge the fact that there has not been a unified vision of the ultimate context that has shaped christology. For example, the metaphysical vision that underlay the christological use of the title "Messiah" in the context of Jewish history and thought is different from the metaphysics that informed the christological formulation of the Council of Chalcedon in 451 C.E. Similarly, the metaphysics that shapes the christology of John Cobb—the White-headian vision of the ultimate context—is different from these other two and is not the same as that which informs, for example, Karl Rahner's christological enterprise.[6] Clearly, then, christology is not limited or tied down to any particular vision of the ultimate context.

At the same time, christology cannot be built on a metaphysical vision that cannot sustain and support the main factors in the import of Jesus. Thus the question to be asked is whether the Saiva Siddhanta vision of the ultimate context is able to sustain and support the kind of portrait of Jesus outlined in chapter 4. Evidently, there are several problems here. I will mention two of them.

The first problem has to do with Saiva Siddhanta's preoccupation with the "soul." The Saiva Siddhanta vision of the ultimate context revolves around the fact that souls, which are eternal, assume different bodies while in a state of bondage, and that salvation or freedom is to escape from the cycle of births and live in close union with God. This means that the concept of salvation according to Saiva Siddhanta is one that lays a heavy emphasis on the liberation of souls from bodily existence to reach the feet of God. This does not imply, however, that bodily existence is seen in purely negative terms. There is a positive evaluation of the physical existence of humans, for example, in viewing it as an instrument of grace for the achievement of salvation. The creation of the world by God is seen as an act of grace by God to provide a context for the process of freeing oneself from the three impurities, namely, *anavam* (egocentricity), *karma* (action-result complex), and *maya* (matter). Yet on the whole, the priority of the soul over matter makes salvation a largely "spiritual" affair.

In christology, on the other hand, there is a deliberate emphasis on the historical understanding of the human and of human salvation. The rule of God as preached, inaugurated, and enacted by Jesus is one that sees the human as being "under" God and "with" other humans here on this very earth. Its goal is not a mystical, spiritual, and other-worldly union with God. The Nazareth manifesto of Jesus is concerned precisely with the liberation of the oppressed and suffering people of this world; the liberated mode of existence is meant for this earthly, bodily existence (Luke 4:16ff.). Therefore when one ascribes the title "guru" to Jesus, there is a danger of understanding Jesus' salvific efficacy largely in "spiritual" terms, something which contradicts the main thrust of Jesus' significance. Moreover, this will also mitigate the traditional importance christology assigns to life here on this very earth.[7]

The second problem is concerned with Saiva Siddhanta's inherent potential for legitimating the existing structures of hierarchy, oppression, and domination in society. This is closely related to the problem mentioned earlier, namely, the excessive preoccupation with the "soul." Saiva Siddhanta classifies souls into three groups, *vinnanakalar, piralayakalar,* and *sakalar,* arranged in a hierarchical manner. This arrangement is based on the idea that souls are eternal and that they assume bodies in several forms in several births. It is only the *sakalars* who need a human guru as an enabler in their salvation process. But interestingly, the two other classes of souls are not historical human beings. So all human beings who inhabit this earth are *sakalars* (*sakalar* literally means "all people" in secular Tamil) and they all need a guru for the attainment of salvation. If Saiva Siddhanta were to stop with this classification alone, it might not pose a problem for a christology that attempts to portray Jesus as the guru for all.

But Saiva Siddhanta does not stop with this classification. In spite of its professed protest against caste, it does operate within the caste system and classifies humans further according to different stages in the salvation process. One's position in the caste hierarchy is often attributed to what one did in one's previous birth. The bhakti poets were articulate in challenging caste and themselves represented a wide range of positions in the caste structure. But this questioning of caste did not result in any structural changes, probably because their religious visions were founded on the Saiva Siddhanta view of the ultimate context. As M. N. Srinivas, a leading Indian sociologist, remarks:

> It is necessary to stress that the mobility characteristic of caste in the traditional period resulted only in *positional* changes for particular castes or sections of castes, and did not lead to a *structural* change. That is, while individual castes moved up and down, the structure remained the same. It was only in the literature of the medieval Bhakti (literally, devotion to a personal god) movement that the idea of inequality was challenged. A few sects even recruited followers from several castes in their early evangelical phase, but gradually either the sect became an endogamous unit or endogamy continued to be an attribute of each caste within the sect.[8]

Moreover, in its elaborate system of *diksa,* or initiatory process, Saiva Siddhanta legitimates the caste structure by prescribing different forms of initiation for different groups within the caste system. Women, children, and lower-caste people are either left out of the initiation process or prescribed inferior forms of initiation. Though the definition of guru is not dependent on the guru's belonging to a particular caste, the disciples are classified hierarchically. The idea of hierarchy is a problem for christology mainly because the community of disciples inaugurated by Jesus the guru is a community of peace and justice, of love and reconciliation. As Paul says, "There is no longer Jew or Greek, there is no longer slave or free, there is no longer male and female; for all of you are one in Christ Jesus" (Gal. 3:28).

I have mentioned two of the problems involved in the Saiva Siddhanta vision of the ultimate context to illustrate how the ascription of the title "guru" to Jesus involves a critique of Saiva Siddhanta metaphysics. But I should be clear about the basis on which I question the adequacy of the metaphysical vision of Saiva Siddhanta. Liberation christologies have maintained that orthopraxis is the overriding criterion by which one should measure the relevance and adequacy of a particular christological formulation. The same criterion should be employed in my critique of Saiva Siddhanta. This is fitting because one of the primary functions of a world view is to provide an orientation for human life. As Geertz points out, metaphysics or world view never operates in isolation from moral and ethical conduct. It is a combination of both. So a religious vision of the ultimate context is never "merely metaphysics" and "is never merely ethics either."[9] According to Geertz, "Whatever else religion may be, it is in part an attempt . . . to conserve the fund of general meanings in terms of which each individual interprets his [or her] experience and organizes his [or her] conduct."[10] Thus my critique of the Saiva Siddhanta world view must be based on orthopraxis. Because a thoroughgoing critique of the Saiva Siddhanta vision of the ultimate context is beyond the scope of this book, I will mention only the kind of questions one needs to ask when engaging in such a critique.

I will question the adequacy and fruitfulness of the Saiva Siddhanta metaphysics on the following lines: Does this picture of the ultimate context adequately serve to explain the various aspects of human existence as we understand it today? Does it have the potential for social and political transformation that leads to a more fully humane society? Does it adequately portray the problem of the human, or does it elevate the problem to a transhistorical level and thus explain away the harsh realities of human oppression and bondage here on earth? Does this vision take seriously the relativizing aspect of the concept of God when it assigns the status of eternal verities to soul and bondage? To what kind of social ordering has this vision contributed in its history? Given that it does provide an orientation for human life, what is the vision of a life that is fulfilling and humane according to this system? Can one endorse such a vision in the particular historical context of today? This particular set of questions does not imply that we are ultimately led to reject the use of guru as a christological title. It only points to the correctives that need to be brought into the concept of guru, enabling us to move on to discover other possibilities within this concept.

LIBERATION AND CONVERSATION: POSSIBILITIES AND PROBLEMS

The present sociopolitical situation in India is one in which the gap between the rich and the poor is so wide that more than half the population of India lives below the poverty-line. This situation of inequality and unjust distribution of resources has led to a growing awareness of the need to awaken the consciousness of the oppressed groups within society for organized social and political action with the goal of establishing a more fully humane society in India. C. T. Kurien, one of the leading economists in India, has this to say:

> A plan to fight poverty does not rely mainly on technical competence. Neither can it be the product of mere formal exercises. It begins with the awareness that a fight against poverty is in the first instance a fight against the power of the beneficiaries of the plans to accelerate "growth." . . . The challenge in the fight against poverty is to mobilize the masses against such a mighty combination of powers and principalities.[11]

The idea of mobilizing the masses for bringing about social change is one that is gaining acceptance both within the church in India and within the society at large. Saral Chatterji, a social thinker and the director of the Christian Institute for the Study of Religion and Society, reports:

> In recent years a new phenomenon in the field of social action has been the emerging style of the struggle for social justice inherent in the life and work of small groups in their local and concrete situations. Both in this country [India] and elsewhere in Asia these groups have been active among the urban and rural poor, organizing them for action against a variety of specific injustices as well as for the certain proximate goal of realizing people's power.[12]

Nor is such mobilization of the poor and exploited peculiar to India. In every part of the globe, those who are unjustly treated need to organize themselves into groups for both social and political action. For example, the homeless in the larger cities in the United States should be alerted to the need and mobilized for action against unjust distribution of resources. The kind of mobilization mentioned here does involve searching for religious and cultural foundations for such a move.

Here the vision of Jesus as guru has its relevance. The idea of guru in Saiva Siddhanta envisions the guru mainly as one who enables humans to acquire knowledge of the self and all else. Knowledge *(jnana)* is seen as the crucial factor in the process of salvation. Though this knowledge is very often seen as esoteric and purely religious, in the christological context it can be given a wider, sociopolitical meaning. However, before I examine how this can be done, I need to face a possible objection. Does not the concept of guru contain the idea of absolute and unquestioning obedience that is required of a disciple by a guru? Is it not the case that such an unquestioning obedience will mitigate the creative self-consciousness to which I have referred?

The authoritarian character of Indian education all through the centuries and even today is illustrative of this problem. The way some of the Hindu gurus in the West have demanded unquestioning obedience also illustrates this difficulty. Writing on the status of education in India, Gabrielle Dietrich, a historian of religions, says that the democratization of the learning process "is probably the most difficult and most urgent task in revolutionizing the educational system" in India today.[13] She writes:

> In India one of the main problems imposed by its cultural and religious heritage is, in fact, that the guru-sishya relationship, which served to transmit esoteric sacred knowledge, is a process of initiation, while the democratic learning process tries to induce functional secular knowledge in a mutual learning process between equals.[14]

While acknowledging the authoritarian character of Indian education, Dietrich goes on to add that it is not "necessarily inherent in the traditional guru-sishya relationship which was a living unity comprehending every minute of daily life."[15] This means that there are possibilities within the concept of guru for bringing correctives to the traditional view of guru as demanding absolute obedience. In exploring these possibilities, a distinction should be made between the popular and the reflective understandings of guru. In popular Hinduism the idea of absolute obedience is predominant, as I noted in chapter 2. The guru is often portrayed as one who is beyond all questioning. Most of the popular guru movements operate with this idea,[16] and that is the kind of guruship we find among the Hindu gurus in the West as well. However, the reflective tradition within

Saiva Siddhanta does not explicitly recommend such an obedience. It mainly advocates a worshipful devotion to the guru. This lack of any explicit reference to the idea of absolute obedience gives room for a democratic understanding of the guru-sisya relationship. Moreover, the fact that the guruship of the guru is dependent on the imaginative vision of the disciples turns the guru-sisya relation into a relation of mutual dependence. This can tone down the authoritarian character of this relationship.

The christological use of guru can bring in several of the correctives needed at this point. For one, the pedagogy of Jesus is one of loving invitation and gentle persuasion. It was founded not on any extraneous authority but on Jesus' own identification with those whom he taught. As Dorothee Soelle writes:

> Identification is the readiness to accept without conditions. It means acceptance as a matter of course. But is there in this disenchanted world a pattern of such identification with another—one which includes the elements of responsibility and risk, failure and punishment, pain and suffering? Such a pattern does exist, but it has been completely mishandled in theology and almost changed out of recognition by controversy. It is the pattern of the teacher [guru].[17]

It is this kind of guru whom I encounter in the portrait of Jesus. Soelle continues,

> Jesus' sayings about himself are far outnumbered by the host of sayings about the kingdom. This is the mark of a true teacher. He does not push himself, his own person, the need for loyalty to himself, into the center, however true it may be that such loyalty follows precisely when it is not insisted on. What is binding on his followers is his cause, his kingdom.[18]

The idea that what matters most in the concept of guru is the new order of relationship—the guru-sisya relationship—reiterates this idea of identification with one another.

Another corrective available within the christological use of guru is the vision of a crucified guru—a guru who suffers with and for the disciples. I have noted how the cross functions as the central symbol of the guruship of Jesus. This vision of a crucified guru can clear the guru concept of its oppressive undertones. It is noteworthy that after discussing the need for a democratic learning process in India, Dietrich discusses the idea of "sacrifice" that is required if the poor are to be mobilized in India.[19] She ably shows how Indian economists (such as C. T. Kurien) and political leaders (like Mahatma Gandhi and J. P. Narayan) have appealed for what she calls a "worldly asceticism." Gandhi used the idea of *nishkama karma* (renouncing the fruits of one's action) of the *Bhagavad Gita* as a model for self-sacrificial action. As Dietrich writes:

> To renounce the fruits of one's action, to renounce the personal gains of a privileged position in the society and to work shoulder to shoulder with the poor and deprived, is exactly what is needed, not only from an idealistic point of view, but also an economic one. . . . Sacrifice can be advocated from a Christian, Hindu or Communist background but needs the effort of cooperation to make the various attempts more fruitful.[20]

Approaching the problem from a Christian standpoint, guru christology can provide an adequate model for self-sacrifice and thus provide safeguards against an authoritarian understanding of guru.

The idea of a self-sacrificing guru, though not found in the reflective traditions within Saivism, is not entirely foreign to them. The narrative and mythological literature within the tradition does have a vision of God's suffering with and for humans in times of crisis. For example, *Tiruvilaiyatalpuranam* includes several stories of Sivam's assuming the role of a humble and lowly human to assist certain individuals who appealed to Sivam for help. Sivam's appearing in the form of a lowly disciple of a court poet in Madurai and saving the poet in face of a challenge posed to him by another poet from a neighboring country is one such story.[21] The mythology concerning the great sacrifice Sivam made in drinking the poison that emerged when the gods in heaven were churning the primordial ocean to get the nectar of immortality is another story, one that is foremost in the minds of the Saivites.[22] It is said that as Sivam drank the poison his throat turned blue and from then on he had been known as *Nilakandan* (the one with a blue throat). This heroic act is seen as "a gracious memorial of his [Siva's] voluntary sufferings."[23]

Though the idea of a suffering Sivam is prominent in the mythological writings, it has not found a place in the explication of the
concept of guru in the philosophical writings. Guru christology can
help bring a creative synthesis of these two traditions in the figure of
Jesus as a crucified guru. In relation to the Christian community, the
vision of a guru who identifies with and suffers for the disciples can
provide a great inspiration for raising the consciousness of the
oppressed poor. The vision of guru as liberating can also provide the
motivation and strength for meaningful involvement in the mobilization of the masses in India. Moreover, those Christians and Saivites
who are working to mobilize the poor can draw orientation and
strength from the vision of Jesus as the guru. Jesus' praxis-oriented
and people-centered pedagogy is a good model to adopt in the process
of consciousness-raising.

TRADITION AND TRANSFORMATION: POSSIBILITIES AND PROBLEMS

One of the chief concerns of this christological project has been to
take serious account of the communal character of the confession of
Jesus as the Christ. Does guru christology address this concern? It is
to this question that we must now turn our attention. I have already
noted that the christological use of guru has potential for meaningful
ecclesial action. However, the Christian community is defined not
only by its involvement in society, but also by its distinctive worship
and liturgy. This investigation must explore whether guru christology
accommodates and takes seriously the worship and liturgy of the
Christian community. Even a cursory study of the history of Christianity will show that the christological formulations embedded in
the devotional writings and expressions have great power both to
evoke an emotive response in believers and thus to enable them for
ecclesial and social action. Does guru christology have this kind of
devotional appeal?

The vision of Jesus as guru includes within itself a personal and
worshipful devotion to Jesus as the Christ. The Saiva Siddhanta
literature is full of examples of such devotion to the guru. To quote
again one of the poems in *Tirumantiram*,

Illumination is beholding the guru's sacred form.
Illumination is chanting the guru's sacred name.
Illumination is hearing the guru's sacred word.
Illumination is pondering the guru's sacred image.[24]

We have already seen in chapter 2 how the great bhakti poet Manikkavacakar pours out his soul in devotion and adoration to the guru. So the Saiva Siddhanta concept of guru is not an abstract and speculative concept devoid of any devotional appeal. Moreover, within the Tamil Christian tradition itself there are several hymns addressed to Jesus the guru. Although these lack conceptual clarity, the christological use of guru in a reflective and systematic manner can bring such clarity to the already existing tradition and can also operate as a conceptual scheme without losing its devotional appeal.

The idea of personal and worshipful devotion to Jesus the Christ itself holds certain inherent dangers. It can lead to idolatry and reification. When the Tamil Christian poets ascribe a multiplicity of titles to Jesus, they tend to equate Jesus with God in an unreflective and uncritical manner. The phrase *yesuteva* (God Jesus) often assigned to Jesus can very easily lead to "christolatry."

The concept of guru, however, has built-in safeguards against such christolatry. The guru concept explicates the guru's relation to God in strictly functional terms. We noticed in our survey of the christological use of guru in India that Indian Christian theologians most often rejected the christological use of guru because their christologies were tied to substantialist language that uses terms such as "nature" and "substance" to explicate Jesus' relation to God. Such substantialist language has a built-in tendency to equate Jesus with God. But the functional approach of guru christology can help one to move out of such substantialist categories. A functional approach shifts the emphasis from what happens to God to what happens to the believer. Thus guru christology is able to protect one from equating Jesus, simply and straightforwardly, with God, and thus from engaging in christolatry. It is able to do this much more rigorously than some of the more traditional christological formulations.

Moreover, the guru concept of Saiva Siddhanta is presented here as an alternative to the concept of *avatar*. God comes to the believer through a guru and not as an *avatar,* a concept which, though it has dominated christological discussion in India, is problematic for two principal reasons. First, the use of *avatar* shifts the christological discourse to the mythical dimension, because the Saiva mythologies abound in *avatars* occasional or permanent. Even though Saiva Siddhanta rejects *avatar* in its philosophical discourse, it does employ that concept in its mythological language. Second, the *avatar* concept has docetic tendencies. Though the term *avatar* is often translated as "incarnation," it literally means "descent." The mythical vision of God "descending" as a human being often tends to picture the descended one in docetic terms. Thus the popular Christian mind in Tamilnadu envisions Jesus in docetic terms.[25] The humanity of Jesus has always been a problem to the Indian people. They find it easier to accept the divinity of Jesus in docetic terms than the humanity of Jesus in historical terms. Guru christology, on the other hand, offers freedom from docetism because the guru is always a historical human being. Note however that the guru is always a historical human being with a definite theological significance, a significance explicated in terms of a functional relation between the guru and God.

In the preceding paragraphs I have examined the safeguards against idolatry in the concept of guru. One can accommodate a personal and worshipful devotion to Jesus without falling into the error of simply equating Jesus with God. Let us now turn our attention to the other problem, that devotional piety as expressed in Tamil Christian hymns can reify Jesus. The word "reification" comes from the Latin word *res* meaning "thing." Thus "to reify" means "to regard (an abstraction, a mental construction) as a thing: convert mentally into something concrete or objective: give definite content and form to" some idea or person.[26] Reification is the process in which an idea, concept, or image is made into an independently existing thing. Hymns and other devotional material have a tendency to reify the images of Christ into objectively existing things. For example, the Tamil Christian hymns use several metaphors to describe the significance of Jesus. Since these metaphors are used in the context of devotional piety, they have a tendency to become literal and thus picture Jesus as an independently existing "thing." Once they are reified, they acquire a certain rigidity and stifle further creative expression of the significance of Jesus the Christ. For example, the titles used by early hymn-writers have been reified to such an extent that writers today who attempt novel and innovative images for Christ are heavily criticized by Christian congregations. Concepts and images become static and not dynamic. Reification has yet another problem. The ethos of devotion most often demands that the poet or hymn-writer ascribe the highest titles to Jesus. The hyperbolic nature of poetic language always borders on equating Jesus with God. Therefore, when such titles are reified, they eventually lead to idolatry by uncritically equating the human Jesus with God. This, of course, is a much more serious "theological" problem.

Does guru christology have the needed safeguards against such reification? There are two elements in the concept of guru that do function as safeguards. The first element has to do with its relational character. The significance of a guru is intimately connected with the relationship that exists between the guru and the disciple. The guru's significance is dependent on the imaginative vision of the disciples who come to recognize and accept the guruship of the guru. This is why I began my portrait of Jesus in chapter 4 with the encounter between Jesus and his disciples. The guru can never be defined without the disciples. This means that the guru is not "out there," so to speak, as an objectified and independently existing thing; so when one is assigning the title "guru" to Jesus, it is not the individual Jesus, but the guru-sisya relationship, that is significant and decisive. To use the words of Irudhayaraj, Jesus the guru becomes "the sacrament of every Guru-sisya dialogue."[27]

Moreover, the vision of a risen guru places the guru-sisya relation at the center of christological articulation. Jesus the guru is no longer "objectively there." It is the spirit of Jesus, as it is expressed in the community of disciples, which is decisively significant for one's orientation for human life. Thus the distinctively relational character of the concept of guru is a safeguard against reification.[28]

The second element in the concept of guru that can function as a corrective to reifying tendencies is the idea of a multiplicity of gurus. Saiva Siddhanta believes that there were and are several gurus. As we saw in chapter 2, this belief is based on the diversity and plurality of the salvific needs of humans. The guru's dependence on the imaginative vision of the disciples reiterates this idea. Even without a specific reference to Saiva Siddhanta, one can affirm the plurality of gurus, for, in fact, there *are* several gurus. Thus the word "guru" always implies several gurus, as one can clearly see when one compares the concept of Logos, for example, with that of guru. Logos, by definition, refers to a single, unified principle of creativity and order. Therefore, when one ascribes the title "Logos" to Christ, it inevitably leads to a triumphalistic understanding of the finality of Christ. On the other hand, when one uses the concept of guru, the idea of the multiplicity of gurus is unavoidable, because the term "guru" has always stood for a multiplicity of gurus in the Hindu tradition. One can argue that Jesus is the only true guru and all other claimants are false only if one utterly discredits all the Saivite gurus in the history of Tamil Saivism and thus prejudges the Saivite faith to be completely false and misleading. I am reluctant to move in that direction, based on my reading of the Saivite religious literature and my contacts with Saivite believers during the last twenty years. Therefore, Jesus will have to be seen as one of the gurus and not as the one and only guru.[29]

Before examining how the multiplicity of gurus can serve as a safeguard against reification, we must note first some of the problems this multiplicity can pose for christology. One of the dominant features in christological formulations until now has been the affirmation of the uniqueness and finality of Jesus the Christ. Though there have been several attempts at rewording and reformulating this affirmation, basically the stance has been one of holding on to the once-and-for-all character of the significance of Jesus the Christ.[30] What are the problems guru christology faces here?

First, the multiplicity of gurus goes against the traditional emphasis on the finality of Jesus the Christ. But uniqueness, as such, is not a problem, because the very idea of multiplicity of gurus is based on the uniqueness of each guru. "Finality," however, cannot be affirmed in the traditional manner when one accepts a plurality of gurus. This means that guru christology needs to address this issue by rethinking and reformulating the traditional affirmation. Second, one may question whether the plurality of gurus will remove the decisive significance of Jesus from the ultimate context and place his significance at the phenomenal level. Clearly, in this examination of the concept of guru in Saiva Siddhanta, the guru concept developed as part of a vision of the ultimate context of human existence. That being the case, the *multiplicity* of gurus does not remove the guru concept from the ultimate context to a phenomenal level. Guru christology, with its link to the vision of the ultimate context of human existence, can function as a normative factor in Christian theology—that is, as that which informs and determines our understanding of God, the world, and the human. Here the main question that faces the theologian is, To what kind of practical consequences has the traditional understanding of the finality of Christ led in the history of the church? Has it enabled the establishment of a community of peace and justice? Or has it resulted in division, domination, and destruction? On the basis of these questions, the theologian will have to engage in a serious reflection and a critical evaluation of the traditional emphasis on the finality of Christ.

The idea of a plurality of gurus protects christology from reification. However decisive Jesus may be in the religious quest of his disciples, he is not to be seen as the one and only guru for the whole of humankind. This will act as a safeguard against the reification of Jesus, because the finality of Jesus the Christ has traditionally been based on establishing in what way Jesus was different from other saviors or, in my case, gurus. There were some who maintained that Jesus was different from others in kind, employing his miraculous birth, his miracles, his sinlessness, and his resurrection to establish this difference. There have been yet others who have attempted to explicate the difference as that of degree.[31]

Whether the difference is in kind or in degree, such an explication of the decisive significance of Jesus is based on reifying Jesus as an independently existing "thing." The portrait of Jesus the guru presented here is able to protect itself from reification for two reasons. First, the functional approach embedded in this christology lays a heavy emphasis on the guru-sisya relation rather than on the individual (reified) Jesus. What is highlighted is the vision of the significance of Christ, crucified and risen, as it includes the community of disciples. Such a vision does not require a reified portrait of Jesus and his import. Second, the difference between Jesus and other gurus is not in kind or in degree but in pragmatic value. One can affirm the finality of Christ only in terms of its contributions to a set of values that lead to the practical consequence of building a more humane and just society. This can be done only in a setting of dialogue with

125

those who owe allegiance and loyalty to other saviors and gurus. As Duraisingh, an Indian Christian theologian, writes:

> We affirm that Jesus is the Christ for he functions within the Christian tradition as the decisive, life-orienting, life-transforming paradigm. We can continue to affirm this, discovering further and further the richness of the paradigm only as we participate in life in dialogue with men and women of other faiths.[32]

Finally, we need to examine how guru christology can be justified within the christological tradition of the Christian community. I have noted earlier that the Tamil Christian poets themselves used "guru" as a christological title and thus guru christology is a further exploration of such a christological use of guru, intended to bring more clarity and understanding to the concept. Yet I have not discussed how guru christology is linked with the christological tradition of the Christian community at large. One needs to acknowledge that the Christian tradition offers us not a single, standardized vision of the significance of Jesus, but rather a set of diverse and different christologies. One notices, for example, several christologies within the New Testament itself and throughout the history of the Christian community. Given this broad spectrum of interpretations of the significance of Jesus, a christologian has to be selective in highlighting a particular strand as relevant for his or her own context. My choice of guru christology is not justified by issues of contextual relevance alone. Its justification comes also from the fact that the vision of Christ as teacher (guru) is not alien to the christological tradition throughout the centuries.

One can discover that the explication of Jesus' significance in terms of his teaching and enabling role—that is, as guru—is already present in the Christian tradition. In the New Testament, *didaskalos* (teacher or guru) is one of the early titles ascribed to Jesus. Though the idea of guru is available within the New Testament, in the history of the early church Logos christology came to dominate the scene and thus became, to a large extent, the normative portrayal of Jesus' significance. This was primarily due to the dominating influence of Greek thought and philosophy at that time.

The idea of teacher has been used before in christological formulations. Clement of Alexandria, who lived in the latter half of the second century C.E., used it with considerable success to explicate the significance of Jesus. While not the organizing paradigm of his christology, it did play a dominant role in his thinking.[33] Søren Kierkegaard, a Danish theologian and philosopher in the modern period, also used the concept of teacher, contrasting Jesus' role as a teacher with that of Socrates.[34] American Unitarian thinkers also have, in their writings and sermons, highlighted the teacher tradition within the Christian heritage and used "teacher" as a title for Jesus.[35] Thus when we assign the title "guru" to Jesus, we are linked with an existing tradition, which, of course, has been overruled and clouded by the creedal statements of the churches as they are dominated by Logos christology. Thus guru christology highlights one strand within the Christian community's life and thought over the centuries. While it is a tradition that I find relevant and useful in my context of Tamil Saivism, it is also a tradition that can be of great assistance in the dialogue between christologians in the global community.

Christology is not a one-way street, in which "eternal truths" concerning Jesus are merely translated into today's idiom. It is a two-way street, in which christological concerns and the demands of the situation interact and influence each other. The concern for the significance of Jesus brings new connotations and correctives into the concept of guru, and the concept of guru, in turn, enriches and corrects the christological concern, bringing to the surface novel and fresh ways to explicate the significance of Jesus. Such a dialectic can help christology to be relevant to Tamilnadu and elsewhere in terms of intelligibility, transforming praxis, and fruitful ecclesial existence. It can provide an adequate model for orienting oneself for a life that is fulfilling and humane, in both the individual and corporate dimensions of our life today.

CHAPTER 6

THE CHRISTOLOGICAL
TASK TODAY

This study began with a description of the bilingual or cross-cultural situation in which we find ourselves today, and a map of the three principal debates that have taken place in the field of christology in the last thirty years or so. We then moved to examine the concept of guru in Saiva Siddhanta, finding it to be a helpful conceptual tool for christological articulation. Though there were a few problems in such a christological usage of guru, I argued that one could find ways to deal with those problems and engage in creative christological articulation. In this final chapter, I want to retrace our steps and discover what exactly we were doing when we were engaged in this kind of christological articulation, so that I may propose a few methodological considerations for christologies in today's global context. In other words, what guidance does our experiment with the concept of guru as a christological image offer us regarding the nature, method, and function of christology? Finally, this chapter offers a working definition of christology and a tentative list of questions that may serve as criteria for the present christological task.

What I have done so far is to talk about Christ with the aid of the concept of guru in Saiva Siddhanta. Traditionally, "talk about Christ" has been viewed as the unpacking, expanding, translating, or interpreting of the New Testament claim that Jesus is the Christ. This becomes apparent when one notices how books on christology generally begin with the story of Jesus' asking his disciples, "Who do people say that I am?" and then proceed to attempt a contemporary explication of Peter's confession, "You are the Christ." This points to an important fact: the primary interest of christology is not in the so-called quest for the historical Jesus, but rather it is concerned with the confession of Jesus as the Christ. We know that the project of reconstructing a biographical account of Jesus is difficult and even impossible. What we have access to is the vision of Jesus as the Christ. The word "Christ" symbolizes the concern for the significance of Jesus and is itself the most primitive vocabulary that has been employed in the explication of that significance. This is why the reflective articulation of the significance of Jesus and the events surrounding him is called christology, and not "Jesusology." In christology one is attempting to explicate the significance of the vision of Jesus as the Christ, not merely asking who or what Jesus is, isolated from this vision.

One might ask at this point whether the very use of the word "Christ" is itself already an explication of the significance of Jesus. I would answer affirmatively. Yet if it were the case that the statement "Jesus is the Christ" was adequate and relevant for all places and all people in all ages, the main task of christology would be either to repeat the formula or, at most, to translate it into different languages. But interestingly, the Greek word *Christos* has hardly ever been translated in the many languages in which the New Testament has appeared. Instead, it has almost always been transliterated. For example, the word for *Christos* in the Tamil Bible is *kiristu*, which is a direct transliteration of the Greek word *Christos*, just as "Christ" is in the English language. The reason *Christos* has been preserved in its transliterated forms is that in the history of the Christian community this word has symbolized concern for the significance of Jesus. By and of itself, however, this word does not explicate and communicate the significance of Jesus. In its transliterated form it is devoid of any meaning unless it is accompanied by a relevant vocabulary that explicates the significance of Jesus for which "Christ" stands as a symbol. This means that the repetition of the formula "Jesus is the Christ" does not articulate any of the concerns embedded in this primitive formulation. Only when one ventures to answer the question, What does it mean to say Jesus is the Christ? does one begin genuinely to articulate the significance of Jesus. Therefore, christology as an activity that attempts to interpret the significance of Jesus as the Christ searches for relevant and meaningful images, concepts, or metaphors from the local context with which to undertake this interpretation.

We were right, then, to choose the image of the Saivite guru, an image available in Tamilnadu's context, as a means of explicating the significance of Jesus as the Christ. But our use of the concept of guru has led us to see that when we ascribe it to Jesus, our discourse is not simply limited to talk about the individual Jesus, the first-century Jewish rabbi, who lived, taught, was killed, and was proclaimed to have been raised from the dead. It must include the community of disciples as well, because one cannot speak about the guru without at the same time speaking about the disciples (sisya). The very character of the concept of guru in Saiva Siddhanta demands such an inclusion of the community of disciples. Since we have consciously adopted a method of mutual transformation of both the term "guru" and the term "Christ," it is appropriate that we allow the concept of guru to take us in this direction. As our portrait of the crucified guru in chapter 4 makes clear, both the beginnings of the ministry of Jesus and the nexus of events known as resurrection, ascension, and Pentecost demonstrate that one's discourse about Christ deals with both Jesus and the community of disciples. Our christological project has been organized around the guru-sisya relation, rather than simply the individual guru. Therefore the profound significance of Jesus of Nazareth lies precisely in his ability to engender a community of disciples, and in the imaginative vision of the disciples that sees the guru's functioning as God to the disciples.

While our resolve to be faithful to the authenticity and integrity of the Saiva Siddhanta guru tradition enabled us to see a wider meaning for the claim "Jesus is the Christ," the New Testament witness itself prods us to move in that same direction. Theologians today, both in India and the West, are beginning to recognize this wider meaning of Christ in the New Testament. V. Chakkarai, a twentieth-century Indian Christian theologian, in using the concept of *avatar* to explicate the significance of Christ, describes the Holy Spirit as the incarnation of Jesus Christ in the hearts of the believers. He writes, "Jesus Christ is the Incarnation or *Avatar* of God; the Holy Spirit in human experience is the Incarnation of Jesus Christ."[1]

Clearly Chakkarai considers the continuing relationship between the incarnate one and the believer to be constitutive of his vision of Christ's significance. In his most recent writings Gordon Kaufman has highlighted such a wider meaning of the word "Christ." He examines some of the christological assertions within the New Testament and concludes that though there are texts which use the word "Christ" to refer to the man Jesus, most of the christological texts are

> better understood if we take [them] as signifying the whole complex web of saving and revelatory events within which early Christians found themselves; for it was in and through this whole complex of events (not the man Jesus alone) that they had come to realize their new relation to God.[2]

Such a view of Christ as signifying "the events surrounding and including Jesus" (to use the words of Kaufman) helps us to address the problems raised by the debate on the idea of incarnation as initiated by John Hick and others. Guru christology, while offering an alternative to incarnational christology, opens up the idea of the Christ-event as the whole web of guru-sisya relations, and thus enables the continued use of incarnational language within a broader understanding of the symbol "Christ." Thus the idea of incarnation does not need any longer to be locked into a discussion of the "stuff" that Jesus is made of; it can creatively explore the new relations that are initiated by the incarnation of God in Christ.

Though the concept of guru within Saiva Siddhanta mainly opposed the Vaishnavite conception of *avatar* (incarnation), the portrait of Christ that emerges out of its christological usage enables one to use the concept of *avatar* within a wider meaning of Christ.

This widening of the concept of Christ is required also because of the way in which traditional christologies have legitimated the oppression of women. Since the significance of Christ was limited to the individual man Jesus, the maleness of Jesus became a normative category for discussing the salvation that is made possible in Christ and for understanding the normatively human. According to Jacquelyn Grant,

> The doctrine of Christology, from its initial formulated inception has been problematic for women. When taken as a basic christological principle (Grillmeier), or as "outlines of christological language" (Norris), the fact that the church teaches that God's incarnation is uniquely represented in the historical male Jesus, provided for the

predominance of the one-sided christological interpretation through-out the history of theology.[3]

This in turn had serious and destructive implications for the status of women in the church and for the view of the ordained ministry of the church. Feminist and womanist theologians have helped us see the sexist and oppressive implications of ascribing Christic status to the individual man Jesus.

As we trace our experiment with the christological use of guru, it becomes clear that we have all along been talking about the significance of Christ in relation to the events, beliefs, and devotion surrounding and including Jesus, and not simply about the individual man Jesus. With this broader view of the term "Christ" in mind, let me go back to where I began the inquiry and trace it as a journey in five stages. I describe these stages around the metaphor of a tree, a familiar religious metaphor within both the Hindu and Christian traditions.[4]

CHRISTOLOGY IS ROOTED IN COMMITMENT

How does one come to claim a certain decisive significance for the events surrounding and including Jesus? What kind of claim is it? Is it a claim that can be established on the basis of historically verifiable evidences? Or is it a claim that is based on the imaginative vision of a community of believers that comes to assert Christ's significance on the basis of its faith perspective? To begin with, let us remember that a christologian who tries to articulate the significance of Christ is not an isolated individual who happens to come across a set of raw and uninterpreted facts about Jesus and consequently affirms the decisive significance of Jesus as the Christ. Rather, the christologian is one who undertakes this explication inside a community of believers or disciples who see Christ's significance as decisive. So the material available to the christologian is the confession of Jesus as the Christ particularly in the setting of *a community of faith*. As Samartha writes:

One cannot build a Christology on the bare fact of Jesus Christ. Those who feel that such an enterprise can be undertaken fail to recognize that the meaning or significance of a fact has a social dimension without which it cannot be truly historical. To be significant is to be meaningful to someone.[5]

The fact that Christ has some decisive significance for me involves both a personal and a communal commitment. My ancestors became Christians in such large numbers that they rebuilt their town under the new name, Nazareth.[6] For most of them the attachment to Jesus the Christ was a matter of communal commitment. The streets and houses in these villages are organized with the church at the center of the village. Thus the very structure of villages like Nazareth, Megnanapuram (the town of true wisdom), and others in that area of Tamilnadu represents the centrality of the commitment to the significance of Christ. I grew up in such "Christian" villages around Nazareth and I was drawn to a commitment to Christ by simply being a part of that lively and living Christian community. Most of these villages have worship in the church every morning and evening. As a young boy I attended these services, listened to the scripture lessons read, and sang the hymns. Later I came to claim this faith tradition as my own in a much more deliberate manner. Thus my commitment had both personal and communal dimensions. My christological interest is rooted in such a commitment.

A word of caution is needed at this point. Commitment to the decisive significance of Christ need not always spring out of, or result in, one's membership in a Christian congregation. By commitment I mean only a resolve to allow Christ to function as an or the organizing center for one's vision of God, world, and human existence. My foreparents, who converted to the Christian faith from rural Hinduism, were gripped by the preaching of the European missionaries and thus came to a commitment to Christ's significance, which resulted in the forming of a Christian congregation. There were others who chose not to belong to any organized worshiping community of Christians. Yet they took Christ—the events surrounding and including Jesus—quite seriously and reflected on Christ with devotion and care. That is why I have examined the writings of people like Gandhi, Sri Parananda, and Rammohan Roy while surveying the history of the use of guru in christological exploration. A wider definition of Christ allows us to include a wide variety of people such as these who are committed, in differing ways, to the community of relationships initiated by and in the teachings of Jesus of Nazareth.

CHRISTOLOGY GERMINATES IN ACCOUNTABILITY

The roots of christology, thus, go deep into both personal and communal commitment. While christology is rooted in commitment, it sprouts forth into the realm of careful thought and critical reflection only when one begins to develop a sense of accountability to oneself, one's own faith community, and others. Let me illustrate this with a few autobiographical reflections. My commitment to Christ in my childhood and youth was more in the form of what Schubert Ogden calls a "christology of witness"; it had not moved to the level of a "christology of reflection."[7] As a young man I was bombarded with doubts and questions about the significance of Christ and had to find ways to deal with those questions and doubts. Thus the stage of critical reflection set in. When I began my theological study, my concern for articulating the significance of Christ in a way that made sense to me became both essential and urgent. This was one of the reasons why I chose the idea of the sinlessness of Jesus as my area of research during my M.Th. program at United Theological College, Bangalore.[8] The choice of that topic for research was also necessitated by my need, as a presbyter of the Church of South India and a theological teacher, to explain in meaningful terms the "humanity and divinity" of Jesus the Christ, because I was deeply concerned about the highly docetic view of Christ that was prevalent among Indian Christians. Hence this concern was an expression of accountability to my faith community as well.

My research on the sinlessness of Jesus led me to recognize the Spirit christology of Norman Hook as a viable and credible christology for me and my faith community.[9] When I returned to Madurai after the completion of the M.Th. program at Bangalore, I found that the Spirit christology that had added so much meaning to the significance of Christ while I was thinking and writing in English was no longer sensible in the context of thinking and teaching in Tamil. It even sounded odd and almost absurd to say "Spirit christology" in Tamil. While I was struggling with the difficulties of explaining Spirit christology to my students in Tamil, I found myself in conversation with the Saivites in Tamilnadu, a conversation which resulted in my discovery of the concept of guru as a viable paradigm for articulating the significance of Christ. Thus the guru christology one finds here grew out of my accountability to both Christians and Saivites in Tamilnadu.

One facet of the idea of public accountability is intelligibility. A christologian deems his or her christology to be accountable and relevant by considering whether it is intelligible and understandable, and whether it adequately communicates the christological concern that he or she is trying to articulate. This means that there needs to be an agreement between the christologian and those whom he or she is addressing concerning the use and meaningfulness of a particular set of images and concepts. I am in no way ruling out the possible new meanings that concepts and images may gain. The consideration is whether such meanings are within the horizon of understanding of the listeners or readers. The history of christology clearly shows how several concepts and images have taken on new connotations and meanings when put to use in christological reflection. For example, when Christian theologians in India used the concept of *avatar* in relation to Jesus, it no longer had the same meaning it had within the theistic traditions of Hinduism. Yet with all the qualifications that are attached to the Hindu concept of *avatar,* the christological use of this term is still understandable and intelligible to a Hindu audience.

Another word of caution should be mentioned at this point. My concern for intelligibility does not and should not imply that I sacrifice the distinctive elements in the significance of Christ for the sake of intelligibility. Nor should intelligibility be given up to preserve a particular aspect of traditional christology. A creative tension should be maintained between intelligibility and the christological concern. My own use of the concept of guru exemplifies such a creative tension.

In today's interconnected and interdependent world, a christologian is accountable to much more than his or her local audience. As peoples and communities become multi-cultural or cross-cultural, one needs to find categories that can open up the portrait of Christ to people across cultures and languages. Yet the process of accountability must begin with the local and move out from there to the global. More often, the cross-cultural character of our neighborhoods has collapsed the local and global into one. The crucified guru thus has the potential to be intelligible in a local situation and in a global context as well.

CHRISTOLOGY BRANCHES OUT IN CONVERSATION

The idea of accountability can, sometimes, lead the christologian to narrow and rigid forms of apologetic discourse, as we have seen repeatedly in the missionary history of Christianity. Such an apologetic stance stifles creativity and shuts the door to novelty and adventure. It fails as well to respect the integrity of other religious traditions. Therefore, the next stage in the growth of the christological tree is conversation. This conversation has both vertical and horizontal dimensions, quite like the branches of a tree. By vertical I mean the centuries of christological articulation that have gone before us; one needs to engage in conversation with the history of christology. By horizontal I mean the conversation that is carried out between my neighbors and me, both local and global. As a christologian engages in conversation with his or her own community of faith and other religious or secular traditions, christology branches out with full foliage.

Though one comes to see and appreciate the significance of Christ in conversation with a community of believers, one is not bound to any rigidly set formulation of what that significance is. In other words, though a christologian's reflection takes place within the context of a tradition, it is not limited to articulating and defending traditional christologies. The christological formulations of the Christian tradition are not "out there," so to speak, as static and unchanging entities, but rather they are changed and modified as they are appropriated by an individual christologian. In that process of appropriation one's own christological exploration cannot be a mere translation of Scripture or creeds; it must be a redescription or a reconstruction of the traditional portraits of Jesus' significance. This happens in a setting of conversation with the tradition. As David H. Kelsey has ably shown in the *Uses of Scripture in Recent Theology,* theology cannot simply be seen as a "translation" of Scripture.[10]

The vision and perception of Christ's significance by the community of faith in which the christologian is located may or may not be the same as his or her own view of the significance of Christ. Yet the christologian needs to take note of all the varied interpretations in working out his or her own interpretation. I am not implying that the credibility of a particular christology is to be judged only on the basis of its faithfulness to a particular traditional formulation (one of the christologies in the New Testament or the standardized creeds of the church). Nor do I mean that a christologian is necessarily a member of an institutional or established church. The point I am making is that christological activity takes place not only for the sake of the self-understanding of the christologian, but equally for the self-understanding of the community of faith that has come to accept Christ's significance as decisive, and for presenting this significance to persons and communities of faith other than Christian. This requires a community of conversation.

A focus on conversation also implies that christology is a communal activity. This communal aspect should be seen in light of the dialogical or conversational element embedded in christology. When a christologian articulates the significance of Jesus in relevant imagery or vocabulary, he or she is addressing not only himself or herself but also members of the Christian community and others as well. There is always an audience involved in the christological task. For example, the christological formulation of the council of Chalcedon (451 C.E.) was addressed to an audience of so-called heretics and the faithful within the Christian church. It was also, perhaps indirectly, addressed to those who were outside the institutional church. Thus there is a dialogue or conversation going on between the christologian and the people whom he or she is addressing whenever and wherever christological articulation takes place.

In today's context, both local and global, there is an increasing awareness of the pluralistic character of one's audience on the one hand, and of the proximity of the so-called non-Christian audience on the other. This awareness demands that there should emerge several christologies, each addressing itself to particular audiences. It also demands that one articulate one's christological concern in wider and more comprehensive terms. These two demands need not be seen as mutually exclusive, a fact that our own experiment with guru christology well illustrates. While the concept of guru in the form in which we have used it is peculiar to Saiva Siddhanta, it is also a concept that has meaning within a global context. The proximity of those who do not profess a Christian viewpoint entails that one envision the christological task as taking place within a wider context, and not as merely limited to a Christian audience. Christology is not simply the Christian community of believers having a dialogue within itself, but also the carrying on of a conversation with those who do not share their vision of the decisive significance of Jesus for one's view of and orientation to human life. Thus the concern for conversation in christology highlights the branching out of christology into several and differing christologies.

This makes christology provisional and tentative. Conversation is a relational and dynamic concept. One cannot talk about conversation except in relation to a context—to a person, to a group of persons, or to a particular set of ideas or issues. Only in relation to something other than itself does the word "conversation" gain its meaning. For example, a christology that uses the concept of Logos to explicate the significance of Jesus is relevant or meaningful only in the context of a conversation with those who know what Logos signifies. Similarly, our idea of the crucified guru is relevant primarily to a Saivite philosophical context. Since contexts and situations change in time and space, and since one belongs to several concurrent communities of conversation, christology needs to take on different forms and to employ different vocabularies. This makes christology provisional. The fact that we encounter in the New Testament, the collection of our most primitive documents concerning Jesus, not one standardized christology but various and differing visions of Jesus' significance, reiterates the point here. There is no perennial christology that is applicable and relevant to all contexts and all ages. Therefore, all christological formulations, past and present, including the New Testament portraits of Jesus, the early ecclesiastical creeds, and our own vision of Christ as guru should be seen as provisional and tentative.

Once christology is seen as provisional and tentative, it follows that it is a critical and constructive activity. The concern for conversation demands that one critically examine the existing christological vocabulary to assess how far it is appropriate to, and credible within, the communities of conversation today. One may or may not use the images, concepts, and categories that have been employed in the past for one's own christological attempt. One needs imaginatively to construct or use concepts and images that come out of or are related to one's own christological context. The concern for the significance of Christ and the concern for conversation come together in this constructive activity. It is not merely a translation of the categories of the past but the christologian's own constructive task. To quote Kaufman,

> The question, then, of who Jesus is (or was) and how we should interpret him theologically must be entirely and explicitly a matter of *our* decision. It is not something predetermined for us by tradition . . . it is *we* who must decide which [tradition] to use and how to interpret it (or them). Our theology must be our own constructive work.[11]

CHRISTOLOGY BLOSSOMS IN HOLISTIC VISION

So far I have only described the ways in which christological articulation takes place. It is rooted in one's personal and communal commitment to Christ. Such commitment finds reflective expression in and through a conversation that occurs between the christologian and his or her neighbors with a sense of public accountability. In this process I have used the phrase "significance of Christ" to talk about the basic concern in christology. Yet I have not defined or given explanation of what this significance is. The meaning of the phrase "significance of Christ" begins to take shape when we ask about the place of christology within the broader field of Christian theology, and the purpose of christological exploration.[12]

The idea of the significance of Christ contains two main aspects, one theoretical, the other practical. The theoretical aspect is that the significance to which I am referring here has to do with a vision of God, the world, and human existence. The concept of guru in Saiva Siddhanta was itself worked out in relation to *pati* (God), *pasu* (soul), and *pasam* (bondage). Though these three categories do not correlate fully with our categories of God, world, and human existence, clearly the significance of the crucified guru rests on its relation to these three categories. Thus the significance of Christ lies in the ability to inform and shape one's view of God, world, and human existence. The Christ-idea functions as the fourth category in the Christian theological scheme (the other three being God, the world, and humanity). The understanding of Christ both informs and is informed by one's understanding of God, world, and human existence. But Christ's role within this "categorical scheme" is different because it is seen as decisive for understanding the other three. I call this decisive or normative role played by the significance of Christ a *holistic vision*.

The significance of Jesus the Christ is explicated in terms of Christ's decisive role in making clear what the concepts God, world, and humanity really mean. Therefore the task of christology is to discover concepts and images that serve adequately as delimiting categories in one's understanding of the other three. For example, the assignment of mythical titles to Christ often tends to remove Christ's significance from this world, and thus makes it irrelevant for the concerns of humans in this world. Though it might give us a picture of God, it fails to play a normative role in our vision of the world and the human. The early church's battle against docetic christologies (those which doubt the humanity of Jesus, and present him as God "appearing" as human) took place precisely on the ground that such a vision of Christ was far removed from the flesh-and-blood world of humans. So christology blossoms forth in providing us a coherent, logically ordered, and comprehensive picture (or a holistic vision) of God, world, and human existence. In other words, the significance of Christ that we are discussing has to do with the "revelatory" character of christological discourse. Here again, the flowers are many; so the pictures of God, world, and humanity that emerge out of the significance of Christ will be many and varied.

CHRISTOLOGY BEARS FRUIT IN TRANSFORMATIVE PRAXIS

The second formal aspect of the idea of significance has to do with providing a meaningful orientation to human living. This is what I mean by the practical aspect of this significance. In christology one articulates the decisive significance of Jesus as the Christ, in terms of its implications for ordering and orienting one's life—both as an individual and within community. This significance is seen in terms of the vision of Christ being able to

> provide criteria and norms and values with which to guide human preferences and choices, with which to assess human actions and styles of life and institutions, with which to stimulate human imagination toward particular forms of creativity and to facilitate the cultivation of particular cultural and individual potentialities in preference to others.[13]

This aspect is what is traditionally known as soteriological significance. Soteriology is concerned with mapping out the human predicament, the need for freedom from such a predicament, and the way to achieve such freedom through the vision of a "savior."

Thus the fleshing out of the idea of significance is to discover an imagery or a concept that points to and evokes a commitment to a life that is fulfilling and meaningful. Does this mean that I already possess a normative vision of what it means to live a fulfilled human life and then go on to measure the appropriateness of my christological imagery by its correspondence to that decisive vision? The answer to this question cannot be simple and straightforward. On the one hand, each of us belongs to specific social, cultural, and religious locations that form our values, commitments, and interests. One's location predisposes one to a set of priorities and preferences. In this sense, every christologian brings to his or her own christological reflection a certain predisposition concerning what human fulfillment is. On the other hand, one's vision of human fulfillment is never static. It always undergoes change and modification as one is affected by new experiences and novel insights. The dramatic changes that occur in one's idea of what it means to be human from childhood to adulthood clearly indicate the dynamic character of our vision of human fulfillment. Thus here again one should note a tension, of course creative, between what we bring to our christological task and what a christological exploration does or can do to our own predispositions.

The understanding of the significance of Christ in terms of Christ's ability to inspire transformative praxis is highly important today. The idea of intelligibility and the logical coherence within the "categorical scheme" are both related closely to and dependent on the concern for praxis. Why should one require christological vocabulary to be intelligible at all? The only possible answer is that here one is concerned with providing a meaningful orientation for life, and that, at the least, implies that it be understandable to humans in a particular context. The same is true of the concern for coherence.

The primacy of transformative praxis is something that is increasingly realized and accepted within the community of Christian theologians all over the world today. As the American theologian Schubert Ogden writes:

Responsible men and women today are typically concerned not only with theoretical questions of belief and truth, but also with practical issues of action and justice, with the result that what they are prepared to regard as credible [or relevant] tends to have an urgently practical as well as a merely theoretical aspect.[14]

I can provide endless references to this concern for praxis in the writings of present theologians. The Latin American liberation theologies, feminist and womanist theologies, African American theologies of liberation, and others accept the priority of praxis. For example Leonardo Boff, a Latin American theologian, invites us to ask the following questions when it comes to describing the significance of Christ:

In what way does [a particular theological theme] help to explain, maintain and transform [a particular set of historical circumstances]? For whom is a particular image of Christ relevant? Who is helped by a particular theme or a particular type of Christology? What interests does it represent and what concrete projects does it support?[15]

Thus the christological tree is judged ultimately by the fruits it bears. Christology should bear fruit in transformative praxis. This concern has been kept alive in our own construction of a guru christology.

Though I have outlined separately the two aspects of the idea of significance, in fact they are one. There is no theory without its practical implications and there is no practice or praxis without theoretical foundations or presuppositions. Therefore, in christology any conceptual analysis that is undertaken is always and necessarily in relation to its potential for fruitfully orienting human life. Similarly, any picture of practical human living as it is and as it ought to be is a working out of a particular vision of the overall meaning of human life. Moreover, any theoretical construction that is not conscious of its practical implications and consequences is thoroughly unprotected from demonic and destructive distortions. Therefore theory and praxis (or vision and orientation) need to be kept together in a creative tension.

Now we are in a position to attempt a tentative definition of christology on the basis of the above considerations: *Christology is the critical and constructive task of imaging the significance of Christ, that is, the events surrounding and including Jesus of Nazareth, for providing a normative vision of God, world, and human existence, and a transformative orientation for human living.*

This definition describes christology as one's own constructive and critical activity and thus opens the door to multiple possibilities within christology. Once christology is open to plural possibilities, the question of criteria becomes essential. Are all images of Christ appropriate, fitting, or helpful? How does one judge the adequacy or inadequacy of a particular vision of the significance of Christ? Given one's access to the christologies of others in different parts of the globe, is not one required to make judgments? These are very important questions today. Therefore, I offer a tentative list of questions that may guide christologians in assessing their own work and the work of others.[16]

Is This Image Intelligible?

The first criterion is related to the fact that christology is an imaging or image-building activity. This being the case, christology needs to be judged on the basis of its intelligibility and communicative ability. Is a particular concept or image that we employ to articulate the significance of Christ intelligible? This question can be answered only in relation to the audience of the christologian. Once we know the audience we can say whether the concept that we use is intelligible. For example, a christological enterprise that applies the title "guru" to Jesus is intelligible to a Saivite audience in Tamilnadu. After we find that a particular vocabulary is intelligible, we need to ask further whether it adequately conveys the christological concern of the theologian. Is there an agreement between the christologian and the audience whom he or she is addressing concerning the use and meaningfulness of a particular vocabulary? As I mentioned earlier, we are not ruling out the possibility of concepts and images gaining new meanings. The question is whether such meanings are within the horizon of understanding of those whom christology attempts to address. Thus the first criterion of christology is intelligibility and communicative ability.

Does This Image Enable Transformative Praxis?

The second criterion is what is generally called "orthopraxis," a recent addition to the theological vocabulary. Traditionally christological formulations have been measured and evaluated on the basis of their faithfulness to creedal statements of the church; in other words, orthodoxy. Orthopraxis, on the other hand, claims that christological statements be judged on the basis of their practical implications. What kind of praxis or way of practical living does a particular christology point and lead to? is the question here. The primacy of this question is increasingly recognized and accepted by theologians all over the world, because issues of peace, justice, and ecological concern have come to take precedence over issues of correct doctrine or ecclesiastical loyalty today. Moreover, one is able to read the history of Christian commmunities and discern how certain christologies have legitimated oppression and injustice. For example, one is keenly aware how certain forms of christological articulation can lead to gender discrimination and sexist interpretations of God, church, and humanity. Similarly, we are able to recognize how the portrait of a blue-eyed, blond-haired Jesus can promote racism and bigotry. Therefore, the criterion of orthopraxis is an important one in judging the adequacy of a christology. One should note that the sociopolitical status of the christologian does play a role in delineating these pragmatic considerations. But a christologian should be conscious of this and thus approach his or her work by envisioning himself or herself in a wider social context. To quote Boff again,

> Theologians [in our case, christologians] do not live in the clouds. They are social actors with a particular place in society. . . . Every given type of Christology is relevant in its own way, depending on its functional relationship to the socio-historical situation . . . it is produced under certain specific modes of material, ideal, cultural and ecclesial production, and it is articulated in terms of certain concrete interests that are not always consciously averted to. Hence the real question is who or what cause is served by a given Christology.[17]

Thus the criterion of transformative praxis is highly important.

Is This Image Disciplined by Historical Data?

Since christology attempts to explain the significance of a historic person in relation to both the historical human being who lived in the first century and the early community of believers who came to recognize and accept his significance, a certain amount of historical exploration into the earliest documents concerning Jesus—the New Testament—is necessary. These documents contain both historical and mythical portraits of Jesus. They describe some of the historical details of the life of Jesus and employ mythical titles such as "Son of God," "Logos," and so on to explicate his significance. One needs to be aware of the priority one assigns to the mythical relative to the historical. For many today the historical possesses priority, for which there are many reasons. First, in the last two centuries of Western thought a distinctly historical consciousness has come into being. One is able today to see how concepts and images develop in the historical process, which thus become available as *historical* truths, and not simply as "eternal" ones. This means that we need to take historical factors into serious consideration in any exploration of the significance of Jesus. Second, the pragmatic criterion we employ in christology demands that if something is to provide orientation for life to us who are historical human beings, it must be grounded in, and related to, the historical reality of humankind. Third, the New Testament itself gives priority to the historical over the mythical in its christological formulations, a fact confirmed by present New Testament scholarship. As Helmut Koester writes:

> The only departure from which the earthly Jesus becomes the criterion of faith is his suffering and death. All other traditions of Jesus' words and deeds are legitimate, not because they preserve the exact memory of Jesus' life, but because they serve as parts of a theological introduction to the proclamation of Jesus' passion and death. In this way, the church in the canonical gospel tradition remains subject to an earthly, human, "real" and historical revelation which is the criterion of the tradition.[18]

In another essay, Koester tells us that

> the question of heresy and orthodoxy today is extremely important. But it is not decided upon the basis of any established creed as such. Rather it depends upon the humanity of Jesus. It is decisive whether or not we are able to affirm for ourselves the basic facts of his humanity.[19]

The liberation theologians have also invited us to give serious attention to the historical Jesus as one who stood for liberation and freedom. Thus a historical criterion is to be employed whenever one attempts to articulate the significance of Christ.

Does This Image Affirm Plurality?

We have already seen that christology is a communal activity, carried out in the context of a tradition or a community of believers who acknowledge the decisive significance of Jesus as the Christ. The history of the Christian community is a history of varied interpretations of Jesus' significance. From the vision of the early evangelists (such as the Gospel writers) to that of the most modern theologians, one sees a range of interpretations. Christology as a communal activity should be consciously aware of this diversity and affirm its plurality. This does not mean that one should uncritically accept existing interpretations and attempt to synchronize them. Yet one does need to address them in order to justify one's own selection process for highlighting a particular vision as relevant and meaningful in today's context. What I am saying here is similar to the historical criterion I discussed earlier. The history of the christological visions over the centuries cannot simply be bypassed in our attempt to construct a relevant christology.

One's christology must also function with an appreciation of plurality if the multiplicity of christological interpretations in the global context is to be respected. Any image of Christ that claims finality and exclusiveness fails to recognize both the depth of Christic mystery and the reality of today's pluralism. Our own exposition of guru as a christological paradigm should guard itself against the kind of polemics that the Saivites engaged in against the concept of *avatar* in the Vaishnavite tradition. A guru christologian should recognize the tentativeness of his or her own formulation and give room for an incarnational christology to discover its own ways of imaging the significance of Christ.

Does This Image Enhance the Worshipful Devotion of the Community?

One of the features of the community of faith is that its articulation of Christ's significance is found, not only in the reflective writings of the tradition, but also and perhaps more often in the worship and liturgy of the Christian community. The hymns, poems, and other works of art that express a personal devotion to Jesus are part of the christological articulation of the community. They may or may not be either highly reflective or conceptually precise. But if we see orthopraxis as an important criterion for christology, then we need to take this devotional material into serious account, because the praxis of the community is more often informed and shaped by this than by higher reflective and systematic writings. Hymns and poems have a great ability to evoke an emotive response to Christ and thus to enable people to commit themselves to a particular style of life. So christology should attempt to construct a vocabulary that is open enough to include a personal devotion to Jesus. Highly metaphysical, speculative, and abstract concepts may not lend themselves to such a devotional appeal and thus fail to motivate humans for action.

Does This Image Maintain the Priority of God?

Finally, personal devotion and loyalty to Jesus have within them the potential for idolatry. There is the possibility of elevating the human figure of Jesus to the level of ultimacy and of God. So christology, one of whose functions is to define and delimit the idea of God, should be aware of correcting itself over against the demands embedded in the concept of God. One thing the idea of God does is to "relativize" the human and protect it from any absolutization of its own visions and achievements. The "radical monotheism" of the Christian tradition demands such a relativization and challenges any attempt to absolutize human values and norms. As Kaufman writes:

> Whatever else we mean by "God," we mean at least that which transcends the world and all that is in it, that which shows everything finite to be but an idol if it is treated as the object of worship or devotion. Thus the theological criterion of iconoclasm should be employed in every christological reflection.[20]

The six criteria that I have put forward, each separately, belong to a whole and interlock with one another. The uniting factor is the criterion of orthopraxis. The pragmatic considerations bring all the other criteria into a focus. What I mean is this: the criterion of intelligibility is employed not because there is something valuable in intelligibility as such. Its value depends on the fact that any articulation of a meaningful orientation for human life should at least be intelligible, so it can lead to praxis. Similarly, historical rootedness is deemed important because humans are historical beings and their life-styles can be defined and given orientation only amid the historical day-to-day realities of this world. As Samuel Ryan, a Roman Catholic theologian in India, writes: "Emphasis on the historical should be made meaningful by showing in relief the significance of Jesus for society and social change. Otherwise situating Jesus in history becomes unimportant, and history fails to enter truly into the heart of religion."[21]

The same is true of the criterion of community. Humans are not lone individuals but members of communities. It is only in the context of relatedness within a community (beginning with the family) that humans come to realize their identity, and the goal and the style of human existence. In the same manner, the criterion of the relativizing aspect of the concept of God is employed so that humans in their orientation to life may be saved from the destructive and demonic potential of idolatry. As one can see, the criteria of intelligibility, community, historical rootedness, and relativization are all needed because of our interest in finding a meaningful orientation to daily human living. Therefore, each of the criteria finds its focus and unity in the question of praxis, and orthopraxis thus becomes the overriding criterion that informs and brings into focus all other criteria.

Christology is a constructive task. It is the task which images and conceptualizes the decisive significance of the events surrounding and including Jesus as the Christ. This significance is seen in its relation to providing a current and holistic vision of God, world, and human existence, and in relation to offering a transformative orientation for human life. The task is governed and guided by the overarching concern for liberative praxis. What does a christology do to people in their daily human existence? is the question that offers directions for a particular christological project. Such a pragmatic approach to christology implies that one can evaluate the adequacy of a christology only after it is acted out, and after one is able to look at the consequences to which it leads. It also means that one cannot be absolutely sure of the workability of a christology when one is engaged in constructing it. At most one can only project oneself imaginatively into the future and anticipate that one's christology may prove to be a fruitful orientation for human life. This anticipation is not based simply on pure subjectivity, for a christologian's critical analysis of the history of christologies and their consequences can contribute to his or her own assessment of the possibilities in the present enterprise. Moreover, a discriminating study of the history of the present imagery and of how that image has functioned in the culture to which it belonged helps to bring necessary correctives and safeguards against destructive consequences. Still, there will always remain an ambiguity in christology. Only future generations can fully know the consequences of a christological formulation and thus judge its adequacy, fruitfulness, and relevance.

The christologian's fate is similar to that of prophets of the Hebrew Scriptures:

If a prophet speaks in the name of the LORD but the thing does not take place or prove true, it is a word that the LORD has not spoken. The prophet has spoken it presumptuously; do not be frightened by it.   (Deut. 18:22)

Likewise a christologian should always be conscious of the inherent dangers in and the tentativeness of any christology. In this sense christology will always remain a search, a conversation, and an unending task.

NOTES

Chapter 1: Introduction

1. Vedanayagam Sastriar, *Kiristava Keerthanaikalum Puthelucchi Padalgalum* (*Christian Lyrics and Songs of New Life*, Rev. ed.) (Madras: Christian Literature Society, 1988), p. 115.
2. Twenty of my hymns have been published in the hymnbook of the Tamil-speaking churches, *Christian Lyrics and Songs of New Life* (Madras: Christian Literature Society, 1988). Some of my experiments with music and hymn-writing are discussed in "Toward a Singable Theology," *Venturing into Life*, ed. Samuel Amirtham and C. R. W. David (Madurai: Tamilnadu Theological Seminary, 1990), pp. 109-18.
3. Robin Boyd, *An Introduction to Indian Christian Theology* (Madras: Christian Literature Society, 1969).
4. Ibid., p. v.
5. Pandipeddi Chenchiah, *Rethinking Christianity in India*, 2nd ed. (1939), p. 150, as quoted by Boyd, *Indian Christian Theology*, p. 147.
6. David S. Schuller, "Globalizing Theological Education: Beginning the Journey," *ATS Theological Education*, vol. 30, suppl. 1 (Autumn 1993), p. 3.
7. Walter Brueggemann, "Foreword I," *The Globalization of Theological Education*, ed. Alice F. Evans, Robert A. Evans, and David A. Roozen (New York: Orbis Books, 1993), p. xi.
8. José Miguez Bonino, *Faces of Jesus: Latin American Christologies* (New York: Orbis Books, 1984); Anton Wessels, *Images of Jesus: How Jesus Is Perceived and Portrayed in Non-European Cultures* (Grand Rapids: Wm. B. Eerdmans Publishing Co., 1986); Robert J. Schreiter, ed., *Faces of Jesus in Africa* (New York: Orbis Books, 1991); Priscilla Pope Levison and John R. Levison, *Jesus in Global Contexts* (Louisville: Westminster/John Knox, 1992); R. S. Sugirtharajah, ed., *Asian Faces of Jesus* (New York: Orbis Books, 1993).
9. I have discussed this in an earlier article, "The Global-Contextual Matrix in the Seminary Classroom," *Ecumenical and Interreligious Perspectives: Globalization in Theological Education*, ed. Russell E. Richey (Nashville: QR books, 1992), pp. 109-14.
10. I am only describing the present state of affairs in the global community, not making any judgments on the pros and cons of this situation. One may question the value of the *kind* of globalization that is happening in different parts of the world with regard to its ability to promote domination and exploitation of the poor and the powerless by the rich and the powerful. I do not go into that discussion here.
11. Robert J. Schreiter, "Contextualization from a World Perspective," *ATS Theological Education*, vol. 30, suppl. 1 (Autumn 1993), pp. 82f.

12. Robert F. Berkey and Sarah A. Edwards, *Christology in Dialogue* (Cleveland, Ohio: Pilgrim Press, 1993).
13. Ibid., p. 24.
14. John Hick, ed., *The Myth of God Incarnate* (Philadelphia: Westminster Press, 1977). See also Michael Goulder, ed., *Incarnation and Myth: The Debate Continued* (Grand Rapids: Wm. B. Eerdmans Publishing Co., 1979).
15. Hick, *Myth of God Incarnate*, p. 1.
16. Ibid.
17. Ibid., p. 31.
18. Ibid., p. 29.
19. Ibid., pp. 179f.
20. One can read the various kinds of objections in Goulder, *Incarnation and Myth*, especially the last chapter, "A Summing-up of the Colloquy: Myth of God Debate" by Basil Mitchell.
21. Schubert Ogden, *The Point of Christology* (London: S.C.M., 1982).
22. Brian O. McDermott, *Word Become Flesh: Dimensions of Christology*, New Theology Studies 9 (Collegeville, Minn.: Liturgical Press, 1993), p. 285.
23. See Jürgen Moltmann, *The Way of Jesus Christ: Christology in Messianic Dimensions* (Minneapolis: Fortress Press, 1993), p. 40, and n. 4.; and Gordon D. Kaufman, *In Face of Mystery: A Constructive Theology* (Cambridge, Mass.: Harvard, 1993), pp. 374ff.
24. V. Chakkarai, *Jesus the Avatar* (Madras: Christian Literature Society, 1932).
25. Gustavo Gutiérrez, *A Theology of Liberation: History, Politics, and Salvation*, rev. ed. (New York: Orbis Books, 1973).
26. Jon Sobrino, *Christology at the Crossroads* (New York: Orbis Books, 1978); and Leonardo Boff, *Jesus Christ Liberator* (London: S.P.C.K., 1980).
27. Sobrino, *Christology at the Crossroads*, p. 379.
28. Boff, *Jesus Christ Liberator*, p. 12.
29. Sobrino, *Christology at the Crossroads*, p. 353.
30. Lamberto Schuurman, "Christology in Latin America," in Bonino, *Faces of Jesus*, p. 181.
31. John Macquarrie, *Jesus Christ in Modern Thought* (London: S.C.M., 1990), pp. 317ff.
32. James Cone, *A Black Theology of Liberation* (Philadelphia: Lippincott, 1970), pp. 202ff.
33. Laurenti Magesa, "Christ the Liberator and Africa Today," in Schreiter, *Faces of Jesus in Africa*, p. 158.
34. Although I do not supply a list of their writings here, each of these theologians has written a great deal on christology. A good summary of all these attempts with critical evaluation by an African American womanist theologian is Jacquelyn Grant's *White Women's Christ and Black Women's Jesus: Feminist Christology and Womanist Response* (Atlanta, Ga.: Scholars Press, 1989).
35. Stanley J. Samartha, *One Christ—Many Religions: Toward a Revised Christology* (New York: Orbis Books, 1991), p. 114. See also Aloysius Pieris, *An Asian Theology of Liberation* (New York: Orbis Books, 1988); and C. S. Song, *Jesus, the Crucified People* (New York: Crossroad Publishing Co., 1990).
36. Alan Race, *Christians and Religious Pluralism: Patterns in the Christian Theology of Religions* (New York: Orbis Books, 1982), p. 1.
37. Ernst Troeltsch, *The Absoluteness of Christianity and the History of Religion* (Richmond: John Knox, 1971), and *Christian Thought, Its History and Application* (London: London University Press, 1923). See also Sarah Coakley, *Christ Without Absolutes: A Study of the Christology of Ernst Troeltsch* (Oxford: Clarendon, 1988).
38. John Hick and Paul Knitter, *The Myth of Christian Uniqueness: Toward a Pluralistic Theology of Religions* (New York: Orbis Books, 1987). See also Paul F. Knitter, *No Other Name? A Critical Survey of Christian Attitudes Toward the World Religions* (New York: Orbis Books, 1985); and Carl E. Braaten, *No Other Gospel!: Christianity Among the World's Religions* (Minneapolis: Fortress Press, 1992).
39. See Gavin D'Costa, *Christian Uniqueness Reconsidered: The Myth of a Pluralistic Theology of Religions* (New York: Orbis Books, 1990).

40. See, e.g., John Sanders, *No Other Name: An Investigation into the Destiny of the Unevangelized* (Grand Rapids: Wm. B. Eerdmans Publishing Co., 1992); Clark H. Pinnock, *A Wideness in God's Mercy: The Finality of Jesus Christ in a World of Religions* (Grand Rapids: Zondervan, 1992); and John G. Stackhouse, Jr., "Evangelicals Reconsider World Religions: Betraying or Affirming the Tradition?" *The Christian Century*, vol. 110, no. 25 (September 8-15, 1993), pp. 858-65.
41. For example, Alan Race has organized his book *Christians and Religious Pluralism* according to this scheme.
42. Berkey and Edwards, *Christology in Dialogue*, pp. 24f.

Chapter 2: The Concept of Guru in Saiva Siddhanta

1. G. U. Pope, *Tiruvacagam* (Oxford: Clarendon Press, 1900), p. lxxiv.
2. G. Subramaniya Pillai, *Introduction and History of Saiva Siddhanta* (Annamalainagar: Annamalai University, 1948), p. 2.
3. M. Monier-Williams, *Sanskrit-English Dictionary* (New York: Oxford University Press, 1899; repr., Delhi: Banarsidas, 1981), p. 1216.
4. John H. Piet, *A Logical Presentation of the Saiva Siddhanta Philosophy* (Madras: C.L.S., 1952), p. 2.
5. "An Historical Sketch of Saivism," *The Cultural Heritage of India*, vol. 6, ed. H. Bhattacharyya (Calcutta: Ramakrishna Mission, 1956), p. 63. See also Bridget and Raymond Allchin, *The Rise of Civilization in India and Pakistan* (Cambridge: Cambridge University Press, 1982), pp. 213-17.
6. M. Monier-Williams, *Religious Thought and Life in India* (London: John Murray, 1883), pp. 82ff.
7. The name "Sangam" (assembly or association) is given to this body of literature because it is traditionally believed to have come out of the assemblies of poets organized by Pandya kings. See C. and H. Jesudason, *A History of Tamil Literature* (Calcutta: Y.M.C.A., 1961), p. 8.
8. See M. Rajamanickam, *The Development of Saivism in South India* (Dharmapuram: Dharmapuram Adhinam, 1964), pp. 10ff.
9. Ibid., pp. 18f. See also C. V. Narayana Ayyar, *Origin and Early History of Saivism in South India* (Madras: University of Madras, 1974), p. 101.
10. Vajravelu Mudaliar, *Tirukkuralin utkidai Saiva Siddhantame* (The inner core of Tirukkural is Saiva Siddhanta) (Madurai: Sarvodaya Ilaikkiyap Pannai, 1979).
11. As translated and quoted from *Tirumantiram* by G. Subramaniya Pillai, *Saiva Siddhanta*, p. 8.
12. Pope, *Tiruvacagam*, p. 40.
13. Pranabananda Jash, *History of Saivism* (Calcutta: Roy and Chaudhury, 1974), p. 81.
14. Rajamanickam, *Saivism in South India*, p. 208.
15. *Collected Lectures on Saiva Siddhanta* (Annamalainagar: Annamalai University, 1965), Appendix I.
16. As translated by M. Dhavamony in his work, *Love of God According to Saiva Siddhanta* (London: Oxford University Press, 1971), p. 128.
17. S. Gangadharan, *Saiva Siddhanta with Special Reference to Sivaprakasam* (Madurai: Angayarkanni Agam, 1992), p. 24.
18. This is why I am not removing any of the sexist language in the quotations from either Saivite scriptures or Saivite and other authors.
19. *Sivanana Siddhiyar*, trans. Nallaswami Pillai (Madras: Meykantan Press, 1913), p. 135.
20. Ibid., pp. 136f.
21. Ilamurukanar, ed., *Tevaram Atankanmurai* (Madras: Tiruvarulakam, 1953), vol. 2, p. 983 (translation mine).
22. N. Pillai, *Sivanana Siddhiyar*, p. 139.
23. Ibid., p. 135.

24. Piet, *Saiva Siddhanta Philosophy*, p. 57.
25. N. Pillai, *Sivanana Siddhiyar*, p. 210.
26. Piet, *Saiva Siddhanta Philosophy*, p. 63.
27. Monier-Williams, *Sanskrit-English Dictionary*, p. 623.
28. Some writers within the Saivite tradition add two more impurities, *mayeya* and *tirodhayi*. Since the dominant opinion in the tradition takes only three into account, I shall follow that classification.
29. For example, a poem in *Tiruvarutpayan* reads:
    Darkness hides objects of vision, but shows itself;
    Anavam hiding all else, itself also remains concealed.
    (Pope, *Tiruvacagam*, p. lxxxv)
    Another poem goes like this:
    "My Lady Darkness" has an infinity of lovers, but hides herself
    From even her spouse with strictest chaste reserve.
    (Pope, *Tiruvacagam*, p. lxxxv)
30. N. Pillai, *Sivanana Siddhiyar*, pp. 185f.
31. Ibid., p. 165.
32. Dhavamony, *Love of God*, pp. 213ff.
33. Ibid., pp. 220ff.
34. Joel D. Mlecko, "The Guru in Hindu Tradition," *Numen*, vol. 29, fasc. 1 (July 1982), pp. 33f. See also Mariasusai Dhavamony, "The Guru in Hinduism," *Spiritual Masters: Christianity and Other Religions* (Studia Missionalia) (Rome: Gregorian University Press, 1987), pp. 147ff.
35. Ibid., p. 34.
36. For example, see: *Sivapirakasam*, pp. 167, 231; *Tiruvuntiyar*, pp. 9, 11, and 23; *Tirukkalirruppadiyar*, pp. 33, 66; *Tiruvarutpayan*, pp. 20ff.; and *Sivananacittiyar*, p. 225. All page references here and hereafter are from the two-volume edition of *Meykanta Sattiram*, vols. 1 and 2, ed. P. Ramanatha Pillai (Madras: Saiva Siddhanta Publishing Society, 1974).
37. Monier-Williams, *Sanskrit-English Dictionary*.
38. For example, Sikhism has a well-developed concept of guru. See Gopal Singh, *Religion of the Sikhs* (New York: Asia Publishing House, 1971), pp. 59-68. For a detailed study of the concept of guru in the differing Hindu traditions, see J. Gonda, *Change and Continuity in Indian Religion* (London, The Hague: Mouton & Co., 1965), chap. 8.
39. Tirumular, *Tirumantiram*, trans. B. Natarajan (Madras: ITES Publications, 1979), p. 232.
40. Tirumular, *Tirumantira arul-marait tirattu* (Chidambaram: Tillaittamil manrrattar, 1973), p. 61 (translation mine).
41. Ibid., p. 60.
42. *"Patti patittup paravum ati nalki"*; ibid., p. 198.
43. Ibid., p. 287.
44. Ibid., p. 186.
45. Ilamurukanar, ed., *Tevaram Atankanmurai*, poem 5357. The most recent edition of *Tevaram* is *Moovar Tevaram: Talamurai*, ed. V. Mahadevan, (Kumbakonam: Sri Kamakodi Ayvumaiyam, 1988). This edition is arranged according to the holy shrines that are eulogized in the poems.
46. Ibid., poem 7486.
47. Ibid., poem 6221.
48. *Tiruvacakam* is a collection of 656 hymns arranged in 56 chapters, written by Manikkavacakar, who lived in the latter half of the ninth century C.E. See Glenn Yocum, *Hymns to the Dancing Siva* (Columbia: South Asia Books, 1982), for a biography of Manikkavacakar.
49. Pope, *Tiruvacagam*, p. 1.
50. Ibid., p. 36.
51. Yocum, *Hymns to the Dancing Siva*, p. 194.
52. The following are the fourteen books, their authors, and their possible dates. These dates are according to Dhavamony. See Dhavamony, *Love of God*. Some scholars place these

authors a century earlier than what Dhavamony has suggested. See M. Arunachalam, "A Rethinking on the Date of Meikandar," *Journal of the Annamalai University*, vol. 29 (1975), part A, pp. 51-58. The fourteen books are: (1) *Tiruvuntiyar*, by Uyyavanda Teva of Tiruviyalur (1147 C.E.), (2) *Tirukkalirruppatiyar*, by Uyyavanda Teva of Tiruviyalur (1177 C.E.), (3) *Sivananapotam*, by Meykanta Tevar (1221 C.E.), (4) *Sivananacittiyar*, by Arulnanti (1254 C.E.), (5) *Irupavirupatu*, by Arulnanti (1254 C.E.), (6) *Unmai Vilakkam*, by Manavacakam Kadantar (1255 C.E.). The remaining eight books were written by Umapati. They are: (7) *Sivapirakasam* (1306 C.E.), (8) *Tiruvarutpayan* (1307 C.E.), (9) *Vinavenpa* (1308 C.E.), (10) *Porriparrotai* (1309 C.E.), (11) *Kodikavi* (1309 C.E.), (12) *Nencuvitututu* (1311 C.E.), (13) *Unmai Neri Vilakkam* (1312 C.E.), (14) *Cankarpa Nirakaranam* (1313 C.E.).

53. Meykanta, *Sivananapotam*, p. 100.
54. Umapati, *Vinavenpa*, p. 54 (translation mine).
55. Ibid., p. 54.
56. As discussed above, p. 46.
57. Uyyavanda, *Tirukkalirruppatiyar*, poem 90, p. 66.
58. Ibid., v. 5.
59. Gangadharan, *Saiva Siddhanta with Special Reference to Sivaprakasam*, p. 144.
60. Umapati, *Tiruvarutpayan*, p. 22.
61. Examples of this use of the phrase abound in the earliest commentary to *Tiruvarutpayan* in *Meikanda Saatiram Patinaangu*, vol. 2.
62. Arulnanti, *Sivananacittiyar*, p. 225, and Umapati, *Tiruvarutpayan*, p. 22.
63. Arulnanti, *Sivananacittiyar*, pp. 244ff.
64. Devasenapati, *Saiva Siddhanta* (Madras: University of Madras, 1974), p. 273.
65. Ibid., p. 237. The metaphor that is used is this: It is not easy to shoot the arrow at an oscillating object.
66. There are several other ways to describe the stages in one's spiritual journey. See S. Arulsamy, "Spiritual Journey in Saiva Siddhanta," *Journal of Dharma*, vol. 11, no. 1 (January-March 1986), pp. 37-61.
67. Monier-Williams, *Sanskrit-English Dictionary*.
68. Umapati, *Sivapirakasam*, poem 5.
69. For example, see Glenn Yocum, "A Non-*Brahman* Tamil Saiva Mutt: A Field Study of the Thiruvavaduthurai Adheenam," in *Monastic Life in the Christian and Hindu Traditions: A Comparative Study*, ed. Austin B. Creel and Vasudha Narayanan (Lewiston, N.Y.: Edwin Mellen Press, 1990), pp. 245-79.
70. *Periyapuranam: A Tamil Classic on the Great Saiva Saints of South India by Sekkizhaar*, condensed English edition, ed. G. Vanmikanathan and N. Mahalingam (Madras: Sri Ramakrishna Math, 1985). Yogi Suddhananda Bharathi offers a shorter summary of these stories in prose in *The Grand Epic of Saivism* (Madras: Saiva Siddhanta Publishing Society, 1970).
71. Ibid., p. 17.
72. *Tiruvilaiyatalpuranam—Urainadai*, ed. Mahadeva Iyer (Madras: Amarabharathi, 1965), p. iv.
73. Srinivasacharai, *Philosophy of Visistadvaita* (Adayar: Adayar Library, 1946), p. 523.
74. Clement Marro, "The Role and Position of the Guru and of the Jangama in Lingayatism," *Bangalore Theological Forum*, vol. 6, no. 2 (1974), pp. 28-51.

Chapter 3: The Christological Use of Guru in India

1. This discussion is by no means intended to be comprehensive. I will look at only a few examples representing different historical periods and various types of literature. I depend solely on written materials in my examination. My treatment of some of the Indian paintings of Jesus will rely only on documents written about the paintings. Moreover, I limit my study mostly to the writings of thinkers in and around Tamilnadu, although I do include a few others who have had an all-Indian influence.

2. For a detailed treatment of the history and theology of the Tamil Christian poets, see D. Rajarigam, "Theological Content in the Tamil Christian Poetical Works," *Indian Journal of Theology* 11:4 (October-December 1962), pp. 130-35; 12:1 (January-March 1963), pp. 3-10; 13:2 (April-June 1964), pp. 41-51. See also M. Thomas Thangaraj, "Toward a Singable Theology," *Venturing into Life*, Samuel Amirtham and C. R. W. David, eds. (Madurai: Tamilnadu Theological Seminary, 1991), pp. 109-18.

3. Rajarigam, "Theological Content," 12:1, p. 3.

4. Ibid., 11:4, p. 130.

5. *Christian Lyrics*, 5th ed. (Madras: C.L.S., 1962), hymn 3 (translation mine). The most recent edition includes lyrics by hymn-writers of today and is titled *Christian Lyrics and Revival Songs*, enlarged and rev. ed. (Madras: Christian Literature Society, 1988).

6. *Christian Lyrics* (1962), no. 12 (translation mine).

7. Ibid., no. 105 (translation mine).

8. Ibid., no. 13 (translation mine).

9. Ibid., no. 110 (translation mine).

10. Ibid., no. 5 (translation mine).

11. Ibid.

12. *Christian Lyrics* (Madras: Madras Religious Tract and Book Society, 1891), hymns 131, 132, and 136.

13. N. Murugesa Mudaliar, *The Relevance of Saiva Siddhanta Philosophy* (Annamalainagar, Chidambaram: Annamalai University, 1968), p. 179.

14. *Christian Lyrics* (1891), hymn no. 249 (translation mine).

15. Ibid., no. 251.

16. J. C. Winslow, ed., *Susila and Other Poems of Narayan Vaman Tilak* (Calcutta: Y.M.C.A., 1926), p. 47.

17. Ibid., p. 53.

18. For a detailed treatment of the life and work of Subba Rao, see Kaj Baago, *The Movement Around Subba Rao* (Madras: C.L.S., 1968).

19. Ibid., p. 17.

20. For a fuller list of tracts and books published up to the early part of the twentieth century, see A. C. Clayton, ed., *A Classified Catalogue of Protestant Tamil Christian Literature 1917* (Madras: C.L.S., 1918). There was an equally large number of materials published by the Roman Catholic churches in Tamilnadu, chief of them being the writings of Roberto de Nobili in the seventeenth century. De Nobili's writings are examined in the section on theological discourse.

21. For a study of American missionary activity in India, see Sushil Madhava Pathak, *American Missionaries and Hinduism* (Delhi: Munshiram Manoharlal, 1967).

22. *The Dawn of Wisdom*, J.R.T.S.: General series, no. 38 (Jaffna: American Mission Press, 1841), 2nd ed. Twenty thousand copies of this edition were printed at that time.

23. For an extensive study of the life and work of these poets, see K. V. Zvelebil, *The Poets of the Powers* (London: Rider and Co., 1973).

24. *The Dawn of Wisdom*, pp. 6f. (translation mine).

25. Ibid., pp. 9f.

26. *Select Tracts* (Madras: American Mission Press, 1842).

27. Ibid., pp. 56f.

28. H. M. Scudder, *The Bazaar Book or Vernacular Preacher's Companion*, trans. J. W. Scudder (Madras: Graves, Cookson and Co., 1869).

29. Ibid., p. iii.

30. Ibid., pp. 1-4.

31. Ibid., p. 5.

32. Ibid., p. 14.

33. John Murdoch, *Siva Bhakti: with an Examination of the Siddhanta Philosophy* (Madras: C.L.S., 1902).

34. Ibid., p. 61.

35. Ibid., p. 62.

36. Pathak, *American Missionaries and Hinduism*, pp. 80f.
37. Murdoch, *Siva Bhakti*, p. 51.
38. I look here at two groups of writings. The first group is by Hindu thinkers who have attempted to explain the significance of Jesus through the concept of guru. They may not sometimes use the word "guru" as such, but they work out their view of Jesus with that idea in mind. The word "guru" does not appear in their writings, because they are writing in English. The second group are theological writings by Christian theologians, both Western and Indian, who use the concept of guru as a christological model. My treatment has the modest aim of studying only a few outstanding examples and does not attempt to be extensive. It does not exhaust all the available theological writings that use "guru" christologically. This study helps us see how and why Christian theologians and other Indian thinkers find the concept of guru either an adequate or an inadequate christological model.
39. There are several books written on the life and work of Raja Rammohan Roy. The leading biographical accounts are: Manilal C. Parekh, *Rajashri Ram Mohan Roy* (Rajkot: Oriental Christ Publishing House, 1927); and Iqbal Singh, *Ram Mohun Roy* (Bombay: Asia Publishing House, 1958).
40. M. M. Thomas, *The Acknowledged Christ of the Indian Renaissance* (London: S.C.M., 1969), p. 2.
41. Rammohan Roy, *The Precepts of Jesus, The Guide to Peace and Happiness, Extracted from the Books of the New Testament, Ascribed to the Four Evangelists* (Boston: Christian Register Office, 1828).
42. S. J. Samartha, *The Hindu Response to the Unbound Christ* (Madras: C.L.S., 1974), p. 20.
43. Rammohan Roy, *Precepts of Jesus*, p. xviii.
44. Samartha, *The Hindu Response*, p. 27.
45. Rammohan Roy, *Precepts of Jesus*, p. 213.
46. Samartha, *The Hindu Response*, p. 35.
47. Thomas, *The Acknowledged Christ*, p. 10.
48. M. K. Gandhi, *What Jesus Means to Me*, comp. R. K. Prabhu (Ahmedabad: Navajivan Publishing House, 1959).
49. Ibid., p. 3.
50. Ibid., p. 6.
51. Ibid., p. 9.
52. Ibid., p. 14.
53. Ibid., p. 11.
54. Sri Parananda, *The Gospel of Jesus According to St. Matthew* (London: Kegan Paul, Trench, Trubner & Co., 1898); and *An Eastern Exposition of the Gospel of Jesus According to St. John* (London: William Hutchinson & Co., 1902).
55. Parananda, *The Gospel of Jesus According to St. Matthew*, p. 8.
56. Ibid., p. 89.
57. Parananda, *An Eastern Exposition*, p. 2.
58. Ibid., pp. 31f.
59. A. J. Appasamy, *Christianity as Bhakti Marga* (London: Macmillan and Co., 1927), p. 19.
60. For biographical details see: Vincent Cronin, *A Pearl to India: The Life of Roberto de Nobili* (London: Rupert Hart-Davis, 1959); and S. Rajamanickam, *The First Oriental Scholar* (Tirunelveli: De Nobili Research Institute, 1972). Nobili's writings in Tamil have been published by the Tamil Ilakkiya Kalakam of Tuticorin from 1963 onward in several volumes edited by S. Rajamanickam. The most recent examination of de Nobili's use of the concept of guru in his christological task is Francis X. Clooney, "Christ as the Divine Guru in the Theology of Roberto de Nobili," *One Faith, Many Cultures: Inculturation, Indigenization, and Contextualization*, ed. Ruy O. Costa (Maryknoll, N.Y.: Orbis Books, 1988), pp. 25-40.

61. S. Rajamanickam, "Roberto de Nobili and Adaptation," *Indian Church History Review,* vol. 1, no. 2 (December 1975), p. 85.
62. D. Jeyaraj, "The Contribution of the Catholic Church in Tamilnadu in the Seventeenth–Nineteenth Centuries to an Understanding of Christ," *Indian Journal of Theology,* vol. 23, nos. 3 and 4 (July-December 1974), p. 185. Francis Clooney also maintains that de Nobili's "insight into Christ as guru is an enormously rich one" (Clooney, "Christ as the Divine Guru," p. 37).
63. Cf. de Nobili, *Tushana Tikkaram* (Refutation of Calumnies), ed. S. Rajamanickam (Tuticorin: Tamil Ilakkiya Kalakam, 1964); and *Gnanopadesam* (Catechism), ed. S. Rajamanickam (Tuticorin: Tamil Ilakkiya Kalakam, 1963), pp. 57ff.
64. De Nobili, *Cecunatar Carittiram* (Life of Lord Jesus), ed. S. Rajamanickam (Tuticorin: Tamil Ilakkiya Kalakam, 1964).
65. Jeyaraj, "Contribution of the Catholic Church," p. 185.
66. De Nobili, *Tushana Tikkaram,* pp. 151ff.
67. Ibid., p. 150.
68. De Nobili, *Gnanopadesam,* pp. 85f.
69. De Nobili, *Mantira Viyakkiyanam* (Tuticorin: Tamil Ilakkiya Kalakam, 1963), p. 53.
70. Ibid.
71. As quoted by Jeyaraj, "Contribution of the Catholic Church," p. 185.
72. V. Chakkarai, *Jesus the Avatar* (Madras: C.L.S., 1921); and *The Cross and Indian Thought* (Madras: C.L.S., 1932). These two works have been reprinted in the volume, *Vengal Chakkarai,* vol. 1, ed. P. T. Thomas (Madras: Christian Literature Society, 1981). For biographical details see P. T. Thomas, *The Theology of Chakkarai* (Bangalore: C.I.S.R.S., 1968).
73. Chakkarai, *Jesus the Avatar,* p. 5.
74. Ibid., p. 6.
75. Ibid., p. 48.
76. Ibid., p. 156.
77. A. J. Appasamy, *The Gospel and India's Heritage* (London: S.P.C.K., 1942).
78. Ibid., p. 55.
79. Ibid.
80. Ibid., p. 247.
81. Ibid.
82. Ibid., p. 262.
83. For biographical details and an outline of Upadhyaya's main theological ideas, see: Robin Boyd, *An Introduction to Indian Christian Theology,* rev. ed. (Madras: C.L.S., 1975), pp. 63-85; C. Fonseca, "Upadhyaya Brahmabandav: The Political Years," *Indian Church History Review,* vol. 14, no. 1 (June 1980), pp. 18-29; and Kaj Baago, *Pioneers of Indigenous Christianity* (Madras: C.L.S., 1969), pp. 26-49, 118-50.
84. B. Upadhyaya, "Christ's Claims to Attention," *The Twentieth Century,* 1901, pp. 115ff., reprinted in Baago, *Pioneers of Indigenous Christianity,* p. 141.
85. Ibid., pp. 143f.
86. Ibid., p. 146.
87. J. B. Chettimattam, "Theology as Human Interiority: Search for the One Teacher," in *Unique and Universal,* ed. J. B. Chettimattam (Bangalore: Dharmaram College, 1972), p. 186.
88. B. Upadhyaya, "The Incarnate Logos," *The Twentieth Century,* 1901, pp. 6f., reprinted in Baago, *Pioneers of Indigenous Christianity,* p. 140.
89. Chettimattam, "Theology as Human Interiority," p. 183. For a brief discussion of Chettimattam's theology, refer to Antony Mookenthottam, *Indian Theological Tendencies* (Frankfurt am Main: Peter Lang, 1978), pp. 102ff.
90. Chettimattam, "Theology as Human Interiority," pp. 188f.
91. Ibid., p. 189.
92. Ibid., p. 196.

93. Xavier Irudhayaraj, "Christ—the Guru," *Jeevadhara*, vol. 2, no. 9 (May-June 1972), pp. 241-49.
94. Ibid., pp. 244f.
95. Ibid., p. 245.
96. Ibid., p. 248.
97. Xavier Irudhayaraj, "Discipleship and Spiritual Direction in the Light of Tamil Saivite Tradition," *Journal of Dharma*, vol. 5, no. 3 (July-September 1980), pp. 279-90.
98. Ibid., pp. 289f.
99. Robert Van de Weyer, *Guru Jesus* (London: S.P.C.K., 1975), p. ix.
100. Ibid., pp. 104-6.
101. Ibid., p. 119.
102. Ibid.
103. Ibid., p. 116.
104. Henri Le Saux, *Guru and Disciple* (London: S.P.C.K., 1974).
105. Ibid., p. ix.
106. For a brief treatment of Abhishiktananda's main theological ideas, see Boyd, *Introduction to Indian Christian Theology*, pp. 287-97.
107. Le Saux, *Guru and Disciple*, pp. 30, 108, and 110.
108. Ibid., p. 30.
109. R. W. Taylor, *Jesus in Indian Paintings* (Madras: C.L.S., 1975), pp. 12ff.
110. Ibid., p. 5.
111. Ibid., p. 155.
112. Ibid., p. 11.
113. Arno Lehmann, "A Brief History of Indian Christian Art," *Indian Church History Review*, vol. 2, no. 2 (December 1968), p. 155.
114. For example, Jyoti Sahi, a working Christian artist in India today, has produced an Indian version of the stations of the cross in which Jesus is presented as a yogi. See *Christliche kunst aus Indien: Jyoti Sahi, Der Kreuzweg Des Yogi Jesus* (Stuttgart: Evangelisches Missionswerk in Sudwestdeutschland e.V., 1992).
115. Alfred Thomas, *The Life of Christ* (London: S.P.G., 1948). See also Taylor, *Jesus in Indian Paintings*, pp. 119ff.
116. Jose Nereparampil, "Artistic Symbolization in Dharmaram Chapel," *Journal of Dharma*, vol. 7, no. 2 (April-June 1982), p. 227.
117. Rammohan Roy, *Precepts of Jesus*, p. 210.
118. D. P. Sham Rao, *Five Contemporary Gurus of the Shirdi (Sai Baba) Tradition* (Madras: C.L.S., 1972), p. 46.
119. Samartha, *The Hindu Response*, p. 41.

Chapter 4: The Crucified Guru

1. This conclusion and the ones that follow in this paragraph seem to have the support of most New Testament scholars today. For a detailed treatment of these issues, see: E. Kasemann, *New Testament Questions of Today* (Philadelphia: Fortress Press, 1969), and *Essays on New Testament Themes* (Naperville: Alec R. Allenson, 1964); James R. Robinson and Helmut Koester, *Trajectories Through Early Christianity* (Philadelphia: Fortress Press, 1971); and Van Austin Harvey, *The Historian and the Believer* (New York: Macmillan, 1966).
2. Harvey, *The Historian and the Believer*, pp. 286ff.
3. Xavier Irudhayaraj, "Christ—the Guru," *Jeevadhara*, vol. 2, no. 9 (May-June 1972), p. 245.
4. John 1:35ff. The language used by John in referring to Jesus is not that of the idea of guru but that of the Jewish sacrificial system. But on the basis of the way in which the disciples

    responded to Jesus and addressed him as Rabbi in their first encounter, we can justify our use of "guru" in this context.

5. Note that in this situation of helplessness the disciples address Jesus as teacher.
6. Sri Parananda, *The Gospel of Jesus According to St. Matthew* (London: Kegan Paul, Trench, Trubner and Co., 1898), p. 8.
7. George M. Soares-Prabhu, "Jesus the Teacher: the Liberative Pedagogy of Jesus of Nazareth," *Jeevadhara,* vol. 12, no. 69 (May-June 1982), p. 243.
8. For example, see Mark 5:35, 12:14, 13:1, and Luke 10:25.
9. Soares-Prabhu, "Jesus the Teacher," p. 244.
10. There are several incidents in the Gospels where Jesus addresses crowds consisting of men, women, and children.
11. The baptism of Jesus can be viewed as the supreme example of Jesus' obedience to God's call and his identification with others.
12. Irudhayaraj, "Christ—the Guru," pp. 245f.
13. Soares-Prabhu, "Jesus the Teacher," p. 246.
14. I am aware of the sexist character of biblical language, which repeatedly uses "Father" for God and "son" for humans. Here I use these only to point out the relationship of grace and mercy encapsulated in these metaphors in this particular parable. I am not in any way legitimating such exclusive language.
15. The Gospels attribute a number of miracles to Jesus. I do not explicate the significance of all these miracles, for two reasons. First, the popular notion of guru has no problem accommodating all such miracles, because in popular Hinduism the guru is often a miracle worker. However, I have limited myself to the reflective understanding of guru. Second, the historicity of these miracles is much debated, and to use the miracle accounts would involve a lengthy historical examination, which is beyond the scope of this study. Therefore, I cite only a few miracles as symbolic acts that illustrate the various functions of the guru.
16. For example, see Mark 11:40ff., 5:41, and Luke 22:51.
17. See John 4:1f.
18. For example, see Mark 12:27ff. and 15:1ff.
19. Here again I am guided by our concern to link ourselves with the reflective tradition within Saiva Siddhanta. The question I have mentioned can be interesting and important if one is working with the popular notion of guru. For example, Ramalinga Adigal, one of the Saivite saints, is professed to have risen from the dead, and to have appeared to his followers. See T. Dayanandan Francis, *Ramalinga Swamy* (Madras: C.L.S., 1966).
20. Hans W. Frei, *The Identity of Jesus Christ* (Philadelphia: Fortress Press, 1967), p. 157.

Chapter 5: Possibilities and Problems

1. Hereafter I refer to our christological project as guru christology.
2. Bror Tiliander, *Christian and Hindu Terminology* (Uppsala: Almqvist and Wiksell, 1974), p. 108.
3. Clifford Geertz, *The Interpretation of Cultures* (New York: Basic Books, 1973), p. 140.
4. Ibid., pp. 140f.
5. Ibid., p. 127.
6. See: John Cobb, Jr., *Christ in a Pluralistic Age* (Philadelphia: Westminster Press, 1975); Karl Rahner, *Foundations of Christian Faith* (New York: Seabury Press, 1978), pp. 176-321.
7. I am not ruling out the possibility of explicating the significance of Jesus largely in spiritual terms. Such a portrait is possible for one of two reasons. First, the concept of guru has potential for such a "spiritual" interpretation. Second, the early portraits of Jesus are not entirely free from such an interpretation. Especially the Fourth Gospel, with its mystical overtones, has given room for such an explication among Indian theologians, both

Christian and others (see chap. 3). My portrait of Jesus, however, is informed by the overall concerns for liberation and conversation; therefore, I make this judgment.

8. M. N. Srinivas, *Social Change in Modern India* (Berkeley: University of California, 1966), p. 30.
9. Geertz, *Interpretation of Cultures*, p. 126.
10. Ibid., p. 127.
11. C. T. Kurien, *Poverty and Development* (Madras: C.L.S., 1974), p. 90.
12. Saral K. Chatterji, "Introduction," *Religion and Society*, vol. 25, no. 2 (June 1978), p. 1.
13. Gabrielle Dietrich, "The Educational Situation in India: Myrdal's Analysis," *Religion and Society*, vol. 20, no. 2 (June 1973), p. 17.
14. Ibid.
15. Ibid., p. 18.
16. D. P. Sham Rao, *Five Contemporary Gurus in the Shirdi (Sai Baba) Tradition* (Madras: C.L.S., 1972), pp. 6f., 25, 43.
17. Dorothee Soelle, *Christ the Representative* (Philadelphia: Fortress Press, 1967), p. 115.
18. Ibid., p. 117.
19. Dietrich, "Educational Situation in India," pp. 18ff.
20. Ibid., p. 19.
21. P. Mahadeva Iyer, *Tiruvilaiyadalpuranam—Urainadai* (Madras: Amarabharati, 1965), pp. 70ff.
22. G. U. Pope, *Tiruvacagam* (Oxford: Clarendon, 1900), p. 162 n. 1.
23. Ibid., p. 162.
24. Tirumular, *Tirumantira arulmarait tirattu* (Chidam-baram: Till-aittamil manrrattar, 1973), p. 61 (translation mine).
25. I made a survey of the popular understanding of Christ among Christians in Madurai, Tamilnadu, in 1975; the results of that survey justify the claim here. See M. Thomas Thangaraj, "The Sinlessness of Jesus—Towards a Contemporary Understanding" (Unpublished M.Th. thesis, United Theological College, Bangalore, India, 1976). A summary of the thesis appeared under the same title in *Bangalore Theological Forum*, vol. 8, no. 1 (1976).
26. *Webster's Third New International Dictionary* (Springfield, Mass.: G. and C. Merriam Co., 1961).
27. Xavier Irudhayaraj, "Christ—the Guru," *Jeevadhara*, vol. 2, no. 9 (May-June 1972), p. 246.
28. The move I am making here from the individual guru to the relation between the guru and disciple is highly significant in light of the feminist and womanist criticism of christology. This is discussed in detail in chapter 6.
29. In a sense, guru is similar to *avatar*, which necessarily implies one among several *avatars*. But the plurality of gurus, in contrast to *avatar*, is founded on historical facts, whereas *avatars* are based on a mythical vision of God's assuming several *avatars*.
30. For a brief listing of the various kinds of attempts at reformulation of the finality of Christ in India, see Christopher Duraisingh, "World Religions and the Christian Claim for the Uniqueness of Jesus Christ," *The Indian Journal of Theology*, vol. 30, nos. 3 and 4 (July-December 1981), pp. 168-85. Duraisingh himself suggests a reformulation with Process categories, which he calls "a uniqueness of inclusion." More recently, Stanley Samartha discusses this question in his book, *One Christ, Many Religions* (New York: Orbis Books, 1993).
31. For example, Norman Pittenger, in his book *Christology Reconsidered*, argues for a difference in degree between Jesus and others (London: S.C.M. Press, 1970), chap. 6.
32. Duraisingh, "World Religions and the Christian Claim," p. 185.
33. Discussing the salvific efficacy of Jesus, he writes: "This [Jesus] is the Teacher who educates the gnostic by means of mysteries, and the believer by means of good hopes, and him who is hard of heart with corrective discipline acting on the senses. He is the source of Providence both for the individual and the community and for the universe at large" (Clement of Alexandria, *Stromateis*, Book 7, trans. J. B. Mayor [rev.], in *Alexandrian*

Christianity, ed. J. E. L. Oulton and H. Chadwick [Philadelphia: Westminster Press, 1954], p. 96). In the same work, Clement writes: "The Son is the power of God, as being one original Word of the Father, prior to all created things; and he might justly be styled the Wisdom of God and the Teacher of those who were made by him" (see *Alexandrian Christianity*, p. 97). Clement, with his understanding of sin as ignorance and salvation as "gnosis," was able to creatively use the idea of teacher in the context of the philosophical thought of his day.

34. Søren Kierkegaard, "A Project of Thought," *Philosophical Fragments*, trans. David F. Swenson (Princeton: Princeton University Press, 1962), pp. 11-27. The Socratic teacher serves as a midwife in bringing to remembrance what the disciple knows or does not know. But a Socratic teacher, according to Kierkegaard, is not whom we need and are looking for, because "if the learner is to acquire the Truth, the Teacher must bring it to him; and not only so, but he must also give him the condition necessary for understanding it" (ibid., p. 17). Such a teacher is more than a teacher. The teacher, then, has to be God, who alone is able both to bring the truth and to create the condition for acquiring it. Such a teacher could rightly be called a savior. This savior is Jesus, the Christ. Here we see another example of a theologian innovatively exploring the possibilities involved in using "teacher" as a christological title for Jesus. However, Kierkegaard ultimately rejects the title "teacher" in favor of "savior."

35. For a detailed treatment of this, see P. B. Wintersteene, *Christology in American Unitarianism* (Boston: Unitarian Universalist Christian Fellowship, 1977).

Chapter 6: The Christological Task Today

1. V. Chakkarai, *Jesus the Avatar* (Madras: C.L.S., 1927), p. 121.

2. Gordon D. Kaufman, *In Face of Mystery: A Constructive Theology* (Cambridge: Harvard University Press, 1993), p. 383.

3. Jacquelyn Grant, *White Women's Christ and Black Women's Jesus: Feminist Christology and Womanist Response* (Atlanta: Scholars Press, 1989), p. 83.

4. For example, the *Bhagavad Gita* describes the cosmic creative process in terms of an inverted tree (*Bhagavad Gita*, chap. 15). The New Testament also has evidences of such a creative use of the metaphor of tree; see Matt. 7:15-20; Luke 3:9; John 15:1-11; and Rom. 11:17-24.

5. S. J. Samartha, *The Hindu Response to the Unbound Christ* (Madras: C.L.S., 1974), p. 159.

6. Nazareth is situated in the V. O. Chidambaranar district of Tamilnadu, India.

7. Schubert Ogden, *The Point of Christology* (San Francisco: Harper and Row, 1982), p. 2.

8. The thesis was titled "The Sinlessness of Jesus: Towards a Contemporary Understanding" (Unpublished M.Th. thesis [Bangalore: United Theological College, 1976]). A summary of this thesis was published later under the same title in *Bangalore Theological Forum*, vol. 8, no. 1 (1976).

9. Norman Hook, *Christ in the Twentieth Century* (London: Lutterworth Press, 1968).

10. David H. Kelsey, *Uses of Scripture in Recent Theology* (Philadelphia: Fortress Press, 1975), pp. 185-91.

11. Gordon D. Kaufman, *The Theological Imagination: Constructing the Concept of God* (Philadelphia: Westminster Press, 1981), pp. 126f.

12. At this point I do not desire to offer a full-fledged material definition of this phrase. Since I am working toward a definition of christology, I can offer only a formal definition for two reasons. First, if I were to give content to the idea of the significance of Christ, I would actually be *doing* christology and not *defining* what the christological task is. Second, a definition of christology can and should point only to the broad boundaries with which christology operates.

13. Kaufman, *Theological Imagination*, p. 129.

14. Ogden, *The Point of Christology,* p. 106. See also E. Schillebeeckx, *Jesus* (New York: Vintage Books, 1981), pp. 669ff.
15. Leonardo Boff, *Jesus Christ Liberator* (New York: Orbis Books, 1979), p. 265.
16. One may ask how criteria can be "tentative." Given our global and pluralistic situation today, we need to maintain that the criteria themselves become subjects for examination within the various communities of conversation. Our conversations should include arriving at common criteria, though tentative, to assess each other's christological articulation.
17. Boff, *Jesus Christ Liberator,* pp. 265ff.
18. Helmut Koester, "One Jesus and Four Primitive Gospels," *Trajectories Through Early Christianity,* ed. James Robinson and Helmut Koester (Philadelphia: Fortress Press, 1971), pp. 162f.
19. Helmut Koester, "The Structure of Early Christian Beliefs," ibid., pp. 230f.
20. Kaufman, *Theological Imagination,* p. 269.
21. Samuel Ryan, "Interpreting Christ to India: The Contribution of Roman Catholic Seminaries," *Indian Journal of Theology,* vol. 13, nos. 3 and 4 (July-December 1974), p. 231.